VANILLA

Edible

Series Editor: Andrew F. Smith

EDIBLE is a revolutionary series of books dedicated to food and drink that explores the rich history of cuisine. Each book reveals the global history and culture of one type of food or beverage.

Already published

Apple Erika Janik, *Avocado* Jeff Miller, *Banana* Lorna Piatti-Farnell, *Barbecue* Jonathan Deutsch and Megan J. Elias, *Beans* Nathalie Rachel Morris, *Beef* Lorna Piatti-Farnell, *Beer* Gavin D. Smith, *Berries* Heather Arndt Anderson, *Biscuits and Cookies* Anastasia Edwards, *Brandy* Becky Sue Epstein, *Bread* William Rubel, *Cabbage* Meg Muckenhoupt, *Cake* Nicola Humble, *Caviar* Nichola Fletcher, *Champagne* Becky Sue Epstein, *Cheese* Andrew Dalby, *Chillies* Heather Arndt Anderson, *Chocolate* Sarah Moss and Alexander Badenoch, *Cocktails* Joseph M. Carlin, *Coffee* Jonathan Morris, *Corn* Michael Owen Jones, *Curry* Colleen Taylor Sen, *Dates* Nawal Nasrallah, *Doughnut* Heather Delancey Hunwick, *Dumplings* Barbara Gallani, *Edible Flowers* Constance L. Kirker and Mary Newman, *Eggs* Diane Toops, *Fats* Michelle Phillipov, *Figs* David C. Sutton, *Game* Paula Young Lee, *Gin* Lesley Jacobs Solmonson, *Hamburger* Andrew F. Smith, *Herbs* Gary Allen, *Herring* Kathy Hunt, *Honey* Lucy M. Long, *Hot Dog* Bruce Kraig, *Ice Cream* Laura B. Weiss, *Lamb* Brian Yarvin, *Lemon* Toby Sonneman, *Lobster* Elisabeth Townsend, *Melon* Sylvia Lovegren, *Milk* Hannah Velten, *Moonshine* Kevin R. Kosar, *Mushroom* Cynthia D. Bertelsen, *Mustard* Demet Güzey, *Nuts* Ken Albala, *Offal* Nina Edwards, *Olive* Fabrizia Lanza, *Onions and Garlic* Martha Jay, *Oranges* Clarissa Hyman, *Oyster* Carolyn Tillie, *Pancake* Ken Albala, *Pasta and Noodles* Kantha Shelke, *Pickles* Jan Davison, *Pie* Janet Clarkson, *Pineapple* Kaori O'Connor, *Pizza* Carol Helstosky, *Pomegranate* Damien Stone, *Pork* Katharine M. Rogers, *Potato* Andrew F. Smith, *Pudding* Jeri Quinzio, *Rice* Renee Marton, *Rum* Richard Foss, *Saffron* Ramin Ganeshram, *Salad* Judith Weinraub, *Salmon* Nicolaas Mink, *Sandwich* Bee Wilson, *Sauces* Maryann Tebben, *Sausage* Gary Allen, *Seaweed* Kaori O'Connor, *Shrimp* Yvette Florio Lane, *Soup* Janet Clarkson, *Spices* Fred Czarra, *Sugar* Andrew F. Smith, *Sweets and Candy* Laura Mason, *Tea* Helen Saberi, *Tequila* Ian Williams, *Tomato* Clarissa Hyman, *Truffle* Zachary Nowak, *Vanilla* Rosa Abreu-Runkel, *Vodka* Patricia Herlihy, *Water* Ian Miller, *Whiskey* Kevin R. Kosar, *Wine* Marc Millon

Vanilla

A Global History

Rosa Abreu-Runkel

REAKTION BOOKS

To Margarita, Gehan, Gerardo, Angel and Tim

Published by Reaktion Books Ltd
Unit 32, Waterside
44–48 Wharf Road
London N1 7UX, UK
www.reaktionbooks.co.uk

First published 2020

Printed and bound in India by Replika Press Pvt. Ltd

A catalogue record for this book is available from the British Library

ISBN 978 1 78914 340 9

Contents

Introduction

Ageing though still beautiful and vivacious, Madame de Pompadour, a patroness to the likes of Voltaire and un-equalled influencer of mid-eighteenth-century French culture, could not deny the truth any further: the romantic ardour for her lover, King Louis xv, which once dominated her thoughts and actions, had vanished. She recalled the way in which she had once stirred erotic passions in many a paramour, including the king, by perfuming her garments with vanilla. Thus she devised a plan to restimulate her lost passion for him: she would alter her diet to consume only vast amounts of truffles, and vanilla.

For me, as a child growing up along the lush, sultry ter-rains of the central plains of the Dominican Republic, there was no shortage of sights, sounds and smells to excite the senses and instil an appreciation of nature. It's the kind of backdrop that demands you visualize the intersection between nature's sensual power and everyday life. For me, nothing embodies that relationship quite like the orchid, a flower that perfumes my earliest childhood recollections – the subtle ways in which its scent and appearance charmed and enchanted our household.

I was often surrounded by women in my family who, with little more than a few utensils and a small wood-burning stove, created extraordinary meals and desserts that prominently featured the orchid fruit known as vanilla. Over the years, these remembrances have become elusive and somewhat vague, yet they have achieved a sort of profundity. I recall the way my mother was fascinated by the flowers and attempted, with middling success, to cultivate them in our tiny apartment, an environment entirely unsuited to the flower's well-being; how she acquired and conspicuously displayed a tacky, bright red silk orchid of plastic origins; and perhaps most importantly, how she used a limited supply of ingredients to produce a magnificently vanilla-fragranced Dominican flan, which overwhelmed the senses and provoked unrestrained consumption.

Much like my memories, it seems that orchids themselves follow me around wherever I go. During my birthday dinner

Dominican-style flan.

in the summer of 2018, my family and I sat at a table in a New York City restaurant, and, to my surprise, there was a white orchid beautifully laid out on our table. It appeared to be inviting me to tell my version of its story. My curiosity begins with the question, what is vanilla? The answer brims with contradictions and surprise.

Intoxicating and evocative, vanilla is considered the only edible orchid and is the second most expensive spice after saffron, while its use as an ingredient surpasses that of even chocolate. Vanilla can typically be found in a wide array of goods, including baking products, beverages, medicines, air fresheners, cleaning supplies, soft drinks, perfumes and even cosmetics. And, of course, ice cream. Vanilla is also believed by many to be a potent aphrodisiac and has deeply ingrained connections to and connotations of race and culture.

Yet this tropical, flowering vine, whose sensual secrets have been guarded for centuries and memorialized through legend, is now so commonplace that it has become synonymous with the bland and boring, though its association with orchids may itself be unexpected. Many do not know that vanilla comes from a flowering vine, and vanilla, both in flavour and fragrance, is seldom what comes to mind when we think of the world of plants.

So what, then, does vanilla evoke? When you hear the word, you may think of its modern use as a synonym for conventional or safe, warm and pure. Perhaps the word conjures images of decadent desserts to which it lends its rich, sweet essence. Most of us have its mysterious extract in a delicate dark bottle in our pantry, which we open only when ready to embark on new adventures in baking. Maybe as a child you experienced a rush of joy and anticipation when the glass bottle was opened and one tiny teaspoon overwhelmed your olfactory sense with its confectionary scent, perfuming your

Vanilla ice cream scoop.

entire kitchen with the promise of a spoon lick or a scraping of cookie dough from the bowl before that dessert was escorted off to the oven.

Or maybe your imagination is drawn to the sultry side of vanilla – that seductively sweet aroma you encountered on your first trip to the perfume counter or perhaps as recently as this evening, or its subtle spice mingling with notes of cherry and black pepper at the bottom of your wine glass. Such is the versatility of vanilla, widely prized for its use as a spice that complements and enhances every dish it infuses with exotic flair and fragrance.

Yet the truth is that most of us have never given a moment's contemplation to this precious flavouring, in spite – or perhaps because – of the fact that we encounter it so often in our daily lives. The very word seems to grant us permission to *not* investigate the subject further. Like so many things in life, it is branded mundane because we take it for granted. And the fact is we take vanilla for granted because we don't fully understand it.

Mundanity is the enemy of pleasure, passion, excitement and curiosity. In the culinary world, whether you're a foodie or a chef, these are the core components of any spectacular gustatory experience. For centuries, cooking and sharing food has been instrumental in connecting cultures and promoting understanding. When we respect the hidden life of the food we eat, be it a single ingredient or an age-old family recipe passed down through generations, we open our minds to a world beyond the boundaries of our insular daily routines.

So why am I writing a global history of a spice pantry staple? History spills the dirty truths of even the safest of subjects. It has the power to show us that even our most banal encounters can be transformed by knowledge of the sources of joy and excitement experienced by other people and cultures, past and present. By understanding the complex yet largely untold story of a thing as seemingly simple as vanilla, you can add value to your own interactions with it and watch the mundanity melt away.

The history of vanilla is as delightfully rich as the flavour we know and love. By sharing its full and true story with you, I hope to inspire a new-found appreciation of this sensual spice. In the chapters that follow, I will take you on a journey that starts in ancient Meso-America and ends with the spice's current cultural significance and postcolonial socio-economic implications. With history as your guide, you may find that you can tap into a sense of vanilla's endless novelty and acquire a new appreciation for something so deceptively plain. The more you discover, the more you will feel like a child again with every turn of the page and every time you step into the kitchen from now on.

But first, let's take a step back. Back to the beginning . . .

M.S. del. J.N.Fitch lith.

Vincent Brooks, Day & Son, L.ᵈ Imp

Vanilla humblotii from *Curtis's Botanical Magazine*, 1905.

I
Biology

Vanilla, the only edible orchid, is exotic, mystical and a pure delight to the senses. Its flavour has been commercialized so successfully that it is unimaginable to be without it. Today, consumers buy vanilla-flavoured products and take for granted its sweet aroma and taste. This wonderful bean was once revered by rulers, temple priests and medicinal doctors. It is still set on a pedestal by the well-initiated such as perfumers and those working with it in the culinary world. The general public, though, are less aware that vanilla has had such an interesting past.

The history of vanilla is rich with mythology. The orchid, along with the fragrant vanilla it bears, is much admired throughout Central America. The indigenous vanilla plant inspired delight and gratitude in the Totonac people of Mexico, who believed it was a gift given to them by the gods. The Totonacs explained the divine origin of the vine within their folklore, which was passed on orally from one generation to the next:

> Xanath, the beautiful teenage spawn of the Goddess of Fertility, fell madly in love with the dashing Tzarahuin. Forbidden to marry mere mortals, princess Xanath, unable to become human herself, instead took the form

Martin Johnson Heade, *Hummingbird Perched on an Orchid Plant*, 1901, oil on canvas.

of vanilla vines so that she could always be near her beloved. The Totonacs would henceforth associate vanilla with hopeless and unrequited love.[1]

Vanilla has a lineage that dates back to long before the Totonacs adopted the plant as their own. To better understand vanilla, we must delve into both the origins of its use and its cultural significance. We must know something about its botanical character and the environment in which it thrives, and how, with human manipulation, the vine became the most significant ingredient in the Totonacs' lifestyle.

As we already know, vanilla is a natural flavouring commonly used all around the world. The beans are frequently referred to as pods and grow from a vine identified as the genus *Vanilla*, which belongs to the Orchidaceae family, the second largest family of flowering plants in the world. Vanilla beans resemble those from the family Leguminosae or Fabaceae, but

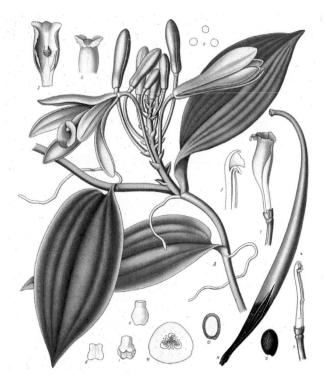

Vanilla anatomy, from *Köhler's Medizinal-Pflanzen*, vol 11 (1888–90).

Orchid flowers and a butterfly depicted in an Oriental style.

they do not belong to that family. The scientific name for vanilla beans is angiosperms, of which there are approximately 300,000 varieties. Angiosperms are the most diverse group in the kingdom Plantae, making up 80 per cent of all flowering plants in the world. Angiosperms all share a common fruit type known as a legume. According to Ken Cameron in his book *Vanilla Orchids: Natural History and Cultivation*:

> Legumes are agriculturally important because of their production of seeds, which include soybeans, peanuts and various types of bean. The traits of the fruit of these legumes are similar to that of a pea pod, consisting of an

ovary which resembles a tightly folded leaf. The pod normally splits into two halves as it matures. Green beans, snow peas, lentils and certain species of acacia are used for cooking, alfalfa is used for its flowers, and indigo and clover are used for their nectar and vanilla is used for flavoring.[2]

Prominent Varieties

It has been identified that vanilla vines have 110 varieties and 25,000 hybrids.[3] The most common variety, *V. planifolia* (formerly known as *V. fragrans*), is grown today in large quantities on the island of Madagascar, and also around the world. The other two well-known varieties are *V. pompona* and *V. tahitensis.*

V. planifolia is native to Mexico and Central America, 'and is known as the mother of commercial vanillas'.[4] The leaves

Vanilla planifolia flower.

Vanilla tahitensis vine.

Vanilla pompona flower.

of the vine are flat, fleshy and produce delicate yellow-green flowers. The beans of *V. planifolia* are believed to be of the finest quality, even more so than *V. tahitensis* and *V. pompona*.

V. tahitensis is a cross-breed of *V. planifolia* and the rarely cultivated *V. odorata*. The seeds of this vine were brought to French Polynesia in 1848 by the commander of the French fleet in the Pacific, Admiral Ferdinand-Alphonse Hamelin. The leaves of this vine are oval shaped and its flowers are greenish-yellow. *V. pompona* is an orchid native to Mexico and northern South America. It resembles the *V. planifolia* variety, but its leaves are longer and wider. The locals named it *la vainilla bastarda*; they believed this specific vine had special powers of protecting the other vines.[5] Like those of the *V. tahitensis*, the flowers of the *V. pompona* are a green-yellow colour; the beans of the *V. pompona* are used mainly in perfumes and in pharmaceutical products.

Growing Vanilla

The cultivation of the vines requires temperatures ranging from 21 to 32°C (70 to 90°F). They require 80 per cent humidity and altitudes ranging from zero to more than 950 kilometres (600 mi.) above sea level. The soil must have good drainage and plenty of organic material with pH values of between six and seven for the vine to thrive. Often the vines require trees (referred to as tutor trees) to assist them with shade. The land where vines are to be planted should provide plenty of eastern sunlight during the day to avoid burning the leaves. The vines also require plenty of weeding so they can feed off the nutrients within the ground. In the Mexican town of Totonacapan in the state of Veracruz, trees locally nicknamed 'pichoco' and 'cocuite' are frequently used as tutors to protect the young and fragile vines, as are corn plants and banana trees.[6] In Madagascar, the Australian pine tree with its lush and widespread branches is preferred for this purpose.

Growing vanilla is fraught with perils that could inhibit the delicate plant's ability to thrive. Rusting occurs when orange-yellow spots develop beneath the leaves, eventually causing the plant to dry up. Overwatering or poor drainage can cause fungus to attack the root system and stems. Fusarium is a fungus that can infest all parts of the plant. This particular fungus was first noticed and diagnosed when vanilla vines began to be commercially produced. Anthracnose, or canker, is a disease that produces dark spots, or sores, which can reduce a plant's yield by up to 50 per cent.

In Mexico in the eastern region of Veracruz, insects such as beetles, caterpillars and other bugs commonly referred to as 'chinche rojo y negro', also known as cobbler bugs, native to the Americas, northern China and Europe, infect vanilla plants with their bacteria as they eat them, causing the leaves to wilt and eventually rot.

In their natural habitat, vanilla vines can climb to the very top of tree canopies. It is not unusual for them to grow up to 24 metres (80 ft) high. The plant has a succulent stem with aerial roots opposite its leaves, which cling firmly to the tree. The leaves of the plant are bright green in colour, flat, wide and smooth. It has a short stalk at an angle between the leaf and stem.

A new vine flowers for the first time after three years and blossoms annually for one to two months. The flowers grow in clusters, and the vine itself produces clusters of around twenty to thirty buds. The vanilla flower has two parts: the stamen, which produces pollen, and the pistil, which contains

Vanilla planifolia vine growing on a tree.

the ovary. Then each flower opens one per day, and about fifteen to twenty flowers open in daily succession. The flowers open early in the morning and live for just one day.

Tim Ecott describes this process in *Vanilla: Travels in Search of the Ice Cream Orchid*:

> The natural pollination starts when the flower is filled inside with tiny seeds attracting small bees. The sticky pollen balls hang above the rostellum, which is a thick tongue flap of tissue separating the mass from the moist female organs. When bees enter the flowers, tiny grains of pollen cling to their legs and wings, which is then transferred to other flowers as the bees continue in their search for sustenance.[7]

Euglossine bee pollinating a flower, Bahia, Brazil.

Farmer's hand opening vanilla flower with toothpick.

Natural pollination of the flowers in Mexico and Central America is accomplished by the Euglossine bee and other small insects. Regular bees are too big to enter into the small flower.

Vanilla farmers must check the vine daily after the blossoming of the flowers and have about twelve hours to pollinate all of the flowers. Pollination season lasts between six weeks and two months, mid-September to mid-December, depending on the country in which the vanilla is grown or planted. When farmers perform the hand-pollination process, they first cut open the flower, exposing the membrane and tissue, then separate it with a small thin stick or toothpick. The male anther is pulled from the female stigma and is gently lifted and pressed together before the pollen can be deposited to the ovary for the vine to bear fruit.

Once the flowers on the vine are pollinated, the bean will grow to its full length within four to eight weeks, but it can take up to nine months for it to mature completely. Naturally, when they are left on the vine, the pods begin to turn yellow at the lower end first, giving off an odour similar to bitter almonds. The pods then begin to split into two unequal halves and a small amount of dark balsamic oil, brown or red in colour, is produced. The pods slowly darken until they turn black. The skin softens, and finally develops the familiar

Malagasy farmer and son inspecting vanilla beans.

The process of maturing of the beans: the bean to the far left is too green; the second and third are turning yellow and beginning to ripen; the fourth is mature; the fifth is over-mature, splitting and turning black.

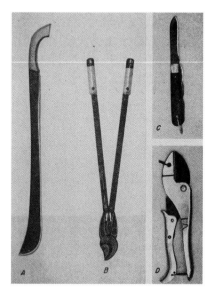

Vanilla-vine cutting tools.

Green vanilla beans on the vine.

vanilla scent. Farmers in Central and South America collect the oil that leaks out of the mature or cured pods and apply it to their skin and hair.[8] You can think of this as a small reward for all the hardships and manual labour the farmers must endure during harvest season. However, other countries sell the oil and package it with the label 'vanilla absolute'.

Afterwards, the plants are checked daily by the farmers. Some of them use a sharp knife to pick the beans, while others prefer to use their thumbs and middle fingers to coax them off the vine. The flavourless beans are harvested green when they are around 15–25 centimetres (6–10 in.) in size. After a lengthy process of curing, which takes several months to complete, the beans become dark brown and wrinkled. Surprisingly, protein, sugars, cellulose, wax, resin, gum, tannin and minerals are all found in vanilla beans.

Processing

During curing, tiny crystals of a chemical compound called vanillin develop both inside and outside of the bean. The wondrous taste and aroma we know as vanilla emanates from this vanillin. Food scientists describe its aroma as 'sweet, balsamic, nutty, dusty and smoky', and much more.[9] There are several techniques used to cure the beans. In Mexico and Madagascar, sunlight is used, which is the ideal way to finish the ripening process. In Java, however, beans are smoked. This particular process of curing ensures uniformly cured beans and minimal bean splitting. Using this method of sweating and drying the pods, the beans will lose up to 80 per cent of their moisture.

Following this curing process, they are then carefully placed on grass mats and laid out in the sun every day for at least two months, but sometimes longer, until they are eventually moved to a shelter and sufficiently dried and prepared to be sold to the local middlemen, for subsequent sale to international companies. In Mexico, producing the perfect beans takes roughly five to six months, though this varies with each vanilla-growing country and region, as they all have their own unique methods of curing. In Mexico, for instance, they typically use oven killing, a process whereby the beans are placed on palm leaf mats inside wooden boxes. These boxes are then placed into ovens for 24 to 48 hours. The beans are then removed from the oven and put into larger boxes with extra leaf mats on top to maintain the heat, which allows them to sweat. This will go on for an additional 18 to 24 hours. Sun killing is a very similar process used by some Mexican farmers, with the exception that the beans are placed in the sun for about three to four hours per day instead of an oven.

In Madagascar and Réunion, on the other hand, the curing process is done by placing the beans in large baskets and

Vanilla beans drying in the sun.

immersing them in hot-water kettles for two or three minutes (the hot water stops the beans from maturing). In Indonesia, the beans are placed over wood fires. This process takes a few weeks to cure the vanilla beans and gives them more of a smoky aroma and taste.

There are a few other methods worth mentioning. In the freezing method the beans are dipped in liquid nitrogen or held in a freezer for a few hours between 0 and −80°C (32 to −112°F). Then there's the Potier's Process, which is a very expensive technique and not in widespread use. It requires soaking the beans in rum for twenty to thirty days before airing them out in the sun for 24 to 36 hours until dried. The beans are then packed up and shipped in the same rum they were originally soaked in. The risk in the Potier's method is that, if done incorrectly, the beans can become mouldy and unusable if not dried properly throughout the process. But no risk, no reward.

Vanilla mojito.

Cured vanilla beans in a basket in Réunion.

Following the curing process, the newly cured beans must be dried and conditioned. The main method for this is rack drying. The beans are removed for conditioning, sorted for quality and then sorted again. Then they are straightened by drawing them through the fingers. The beans are tied into bundles of about fifty, wrapped in wax paper and placed in metal conditioning boxes lined with wax paper. This process takes about three months. The beans are packed according to the different categories and the countries in which they are produced. Appearance is not a key factor; what's more important is the moisture and vanillin content. Lastly, before getting to the market the beans are given a special grade determined by their colour, size, lustre, moisture content, and whether they are without blemish. The grading system depends on the country in which they are produced. The two main categories you will normally see in your local market will be 'A' or 'B'. (This will be discussed further in Chapter Seven.)

As you can plainly see, the creation of this precious flavour is anything but plain. In fact, it can be compared to the human life cycle – from seeds and pollination, taking nine months for the vine to produce the beans, all the way to maturation and its final destination in our pantries. Indeed vanilla's history is our history, and this untamed flavour has charmed the likes of kings and queens throughout the passing ages, no differently to how it continues to charm us today.

2
History and Origins

The story of the vanilla vine can be traced back to about 70 million years ago.[1] The vines grew in the humid lowland tropical forests of the eastern slopes of the Andes, through South America to the Guianas, northeastern Brazil and the Caribbean. In these regions the vines produce beans; outside of these countries they only produce flowers, as was discovered around the seventeenth century. Until recently, it was believed that the Melipona bee was responsible for pollinating the flowers. However, new research indicates that the Euglossine bee, found only in Mexico and Central America, is one of the main pollinators.

The indigenous people most likely found the beans on the forest grounds, became curious about the shrivelled black pods and decided to explore how they might be used. They used the beans as early as 2,000 to 3,000 years before the Spanish conquest of Mexico in 1521. They used vanilla for its medicinal properties and frequently mixed it with various herbs. The beans were also ground and mixed with copal, a dried resin from the copalli tree with a pleasing pine-like aroma, as an incense to perfume their temples during their ceremonies.[2]

Vanilla vines were successfully domesticated in the early nineteenth century in the Mexican town of Papantla, which

Vanilla vines colour insert in the *Encyclopedia of Food* (1923).

John Nugent Finch, parts of *Vanilla planifolia*, 1891, engraving in *Curtis's Botanical Magazine*.

Vanilla beans.

at one time was the centre of vanilla production. Vanilla farming is associated with many Mexican cultures like those of the Totonacs, Mayans, Mazatecs and Chinantecs, among other tribes. These indigenous communities all lived close to one another and traded with each other. The uses and cultivation of vanilla evolved slowly over time among the Meso-American cultures.

Pride in having a lineage of strong, brave and intelligent ancestors was characteristic of Meso-American communities such as the Olmecs, Toltecs, Mayans, Totonacs and Aztecs. Those ancestors left behind methods of cultivating, cooking and flavouring food and beverages that proved vital for their survival. Let's take a closer look at how each of these diverse cultures used vanilla.

Meso-American Cultures

The Olmecs, a group that settled in the areas of Veracruz and Tabasco in 1150 BCE, were the first advanced civilization in Meso-America and are considered to be the 'mother culture' of Mexico. Unlike other tribes during this time that relied on primitive tools for survival, the Olmecs distinguished themselves through technological advancement. They developed

Olmec bench figure, 5th–2nd century BCE, stone.

both an urban planning and a writing system. They are known for their carvings of large stone heads, as well as small carvings of jade in the form of a jaguar, which was their rain god. Corn and cocoa were among the crops they domesticated, and they used both to create a drink called *atole*, which was made with corn and chilli and flavoured with vanilla. In fact, archaeologists believe they may have been the first Meso-American tribe to use the vanilla bean as a flavouring agent. The Olmec Empire eventually disappeared around 400 BCE, for reasons unknown.

The Toltecs, on the other hand, whose name means 'people of the reeds', migrated from the northern part of Mexico.[3] They established a strong civilization that endured from the tenth to twelfth centuries CE. They are considered to be one of the great cultures that existed in Meso-America before the birth of the Aztecs. The Toltecs settled outside of central Mexico and built an empire that extended from the Atlantic side of Mexico to Veracruz and Tabasco. Famous for their military prowess, their most well-known city, Tula (or Tollan), was the manufacturing centre for the production of all the sharp tools and weapons that Toltec artisans crafted out of green and gold volcanic glass. The wealth of the Toltec people came not only from agriculture and commerce, but from duties they collected from their conquered subjects. The Toltecs revered Quetzalcoatl, a god representing the morning and evening star, whose stark appearance, fair-skinned and bearded, resembled that of a nobleman (the Aztecs considered it to be the plumed serpent, the god of wind and rain and creator of the world and mankind). According to Toltec folklore, this nobleman lived among them for twenty years until he was banished by Tezcatlipoca, god of the night sky. It was prophesied that Quetzalcoatl would return one day to reclaim his rightful place among his people.

Toltec sculptures in the city of Tula, Mexico.

The Mayans migrated from the lowlands of Guatemala to Mexico in 1000 BCE, and their empire stretched from southeastern Mexico to northern Central America. In the Yucatan peninsula of Mexico, they built the famed city of Chichen Itza between 400 and 600 CE. Though their empire slowly collapsed amid social and political turbulence, the Mayans are recognized for their development of an advanced society – members of which were astronomers, mathematicians, artists and architects – and their cultural contributions, which include the creation of a calendar and astrological system, as well as a written language, called Mayan glyphs. Their society had a distinct class structure – a class of elites, a middle class that included priests, soldiers, potters, textile workers and merchants, and a lower class that consisted of servants and farmers.[4] The Mayan economy was based upon the development of city-states, each of which was connected to a well-organized trade network. The

Mayan diet included corn (maize), squash, chillies, beans and peppers. They frequently used vanilla for flavouring.

Around 600 CE, a Meso-American tribe known as the Totonacs settled in the south-central gulf lowlands of Mexico, where they lived in small villages nestled among the hills near the Tecolutla River. The vanilla plant, indigenous to their land, captivated the Totonac people. They adopted the vanilla vine, enshrined it in their cultural identity and revered it as a divine plant in their daily lives. This oral legend passed down by generations of elders over many centuries tells us some of what we know about the Totonacs' relationship with vanilla:

> Tzacopontziza and Zkatan-Oxga, star-crossed lovers and born to royalty, fled from a magnificent temple near Papantla at which princess Tzacopontziza served, only to encounter a terrible beast which threatened death if they failed to return. Arriving back at the temple, furious priests murdered the pair, removed their hearts and tossed their bodies in a nearby ravine. At that very spot, a tree miraculously took root, thrived and eventually hosted vanilla vines whose aromatic flowers and tantalizing fruit, the priests and locals believed, derived from the slain couple's blood.[5]

It is no surprise that the vanilla vine had such significance to the Totonac people, given that the territory they dominated, a region historically known as Totonacapan and which falls within the modern state of Veracruz, encompasses the heart of vanilla-growing terrain. El Tajín and Papantla were two historically significant centres within the region of Totonacapan, and both were central to the identity of the Totonac people, who reside to this day in communities within the state of Veracruz in the cities of Puebla, Papantla and Hidalgo.

Totanac mural in the Asunción church, Papantla, Veracruz.

The Totonacs inherited and rebuilt one of the greatest cities in Meso-America, El Tajín. Papantla, which has been called the city that perfumes the world, is the heart of the vanilla-growing region and remains a centre of Totonac culture.[6] The relationship between the Totonacs and the vanilla vine involved a mixture of reverence and practical mastery; it is a legacy that survives in the contemporary outdoor markets of the city, stocked year-round with small decorative baskets, animal figurines and other trinkets made from the vanilla pod by the indigenous population. To fully appreciate how deeply rooted in modern uses of the vanilla vine is Totonac culture, one can visit Papantla in early summer and experience the city's annual vanilla festival, which pre-dates the Spanish conquest.

In Meso-America, great civilizations rose and fell, and one of the most well-known and prominent empires was the Aztec. 'The Aztecs were previously known as the *Mexica* or *Tenochcas*, which were most likely a group of only 10,000 people, who, according to legend, followed Huitzilopochtli, the "hummingbird wizard" and the god of the sun and war.'[7]

Huitzilopochtli, the god of sun, war and human sacrifice.

Similar to the Roman Empire, the Aztecs absorbed other cultures and adopted many of their traits and attributes. The inhabitants of the region who came prior to the Aztecs were mostly hunters and gatherers who feasted on plants. As the groups became more sedentary, they began to depend more on plants like corn, beans and avocados.

It is believed the Mexica migrated to the lake area around 1248 CE, when a group of Nahua people were instructed to leave their homes via order of their god, Huitzilopochtli. The city of Tenochtitlan, which the Aztecs inherited via war, was developed into a modern city with temples, schools for their priests, palaces, adobe residential buildings and marketplaces. The city was expanded into the waters of Texcoco Lake. As the legend goes, the group of Nahua migrants came across an eagle perched atop a cactus while it devoured a snake.

Quetzalcoatl, the great plumed serpent god, was transformed into an eagle and landed on a cactus plant while holding a serpent in his beak. According to legend, Huitzilopochtli had informed his people that they should settle once they came across the site of the eagle. This was the sign for the Mexicas to set down roots around this lake, which was considered one of the most spectacular natural wonders of the world. Thus this is the official beginning of the Aztec Empire.

The Aztecs were the rulers of all neighbouring tribes. One of those tribes was the Totonac people, who, as previously mentioned, were highly skilled in the cultivation of vanilla vines. Once they became the subjects of the Aztecs, the rulers demanded that the Totonacs produce vanilla exclusively for them.

The New World

On 3 August 1492 Christopher Columbus departed Spain in search of the shortest route to Asia; instead, on 12 October of that same year, he arrived in uncharted lands, which would become what we now call the American continent. He carried with him in his ships many products from Europe. He then also transported many products from these foreign lands on the journey back. This began an ongoing exchange of goods known as the 'Columbian Exchange', a phrase coined by the historian Alfred Crosby in 1972. When vanilla arrived in Europe in the sixteenth century, its first use was as an additive to chocolate.

In a rather short time, the Spaniards established several permanent colonies throughout the Caribbean, where indigenous people almost immediately became enslaved. Upon receiving news that great riches awaited in the Yucatán, Cuba's governor at the time, Diego Velázquez, sent the *encomendero*, or policyholder, Hernán Cortés to lead an expedition. When the Spaniards defeated the indigenous forces, they were awarded *encomiendas*, a tribute system granted by the Spanish Crown to a colonist who, in turn, governed the land. The *encomienda* system was comprised of forced labour that depended on the blood and sweat of indigenous people. During his journey, Cortés encountered Jerónimo de Aguilar, a fellow Spaniard who landed in the region after a shipwreck. Aguilar had become familiar with the indigenous language and befriended several indigenous people, who also communicated with Cortés. Although he received warnings not to continue on his route towards Tenochtitlan, Cortés marched on, and subsequently learned of the strife within the different indigenous communities. Cortés battled the Aztecs throughout a bloody three-year period, from 1519 to 1521. When Cortés arrived, the Totonacs and Tlaxcalans saw an opportunity to rid themselves of the cruel Aztecs, who still used human sacrificial ceremonies to appease their bloodthirsty gods.

As told in many accounts, the Aztecs saw the paleskinned conquistadors as gods and for the first time saw horses, cannons and firearms. This particular perspective has its origins in Francisco López de Gómara's published account *Historia general de las Indias* (1552; General History of the Indies).[8] However, as historian Camilla Townsend argues in 'Burying the White Gods: New Perspectives on the Conquest of Mexico', published in 2003, 'the Aztecs never saw the Spaniards as gods, as has often been written about by a myriad of scholars.' In fact, Gómara never travelled to New Spain. Most likely his account was grossly exaggerated.[9]

As the accounts go, the Aztecs and their ruler Montezuma II showered the Spaniards with lavish meals and gifts, only to be ultimately defeated by Cortés, who claimed Mexico for

Spain. Bernal Díaz del Castillo, who kept detailed records of the military campaign against the Aztecs, spent many years writing a full record of the Aztec culture. Diaz published his manuscripts under the title *La Historia verdadera de la conquista de la Nueva España* (The True History of the Conquest of New Spain). The author wanted to ensure that there was an eye-witness narrative of the conquering of the Aztecs, since there were many others writing about it with second-hand inform-ation at the time. It was he who first noted that vanilla beans were originally added to ground cocoa beans, chilli, and corn to make a frothy, thick and fragrant drink called *xocoatl*, which translates as 'bitter water'. The conquistadors found this drink unpleasant and did not understand why Montezuma II drank it fifty times per day out of golden cups. The explanation was that the Aztecs drank this exotic concoction for stamina and virility, and Montezuma II had many wives in his palace to appease.

One of the most well-known figures in Aztec history is La Malinche, or Doña Marina, an indigenous Nahua woman

Book illustration from 1900, of Cortés meeting Montezuma II.

who is often credited with bringing down the Aztec Empire. La Malinche was a translator and intermediary of Cortés. She was one of about twenty enslaved women offered to the Spaniards. She would later bear Cortés his first child. Although La Malinche has been depicted as a heroine by some, including Díaz, she has also been vilified by several Mexican nationalist writers.

During the period of hosting these would-be white gods, the emperor ordered that the Spaniards be shown the city and its temples. In his welcoming banquet they were served fowl,

Sixteenth-century painting of human sacrifice at an Aztec temple, from the *Codex Magliabechiano*.

Orchid plant (*Serapias garbariorum*) with roots, from *Deutsche botanische Monatsschrift* (1912).

turkeys, native partridges, wild ducks, quail, wild boar, rabbits, vegetables and fruits. However, the Spaniards were horrified when they discovered upon visiting various temples that the main altars were full of rotting human hearts, and the walls surrounding the altars were caked in blood. This gave the Spaniards reason enough to wage war against Montezuma II and convert his people to Christianity.

While at the palace, the Spaniards tried to observe the Totonacs, who made one of the ingredients of Montezuma's aphrodisiac drink, which they called vainilla, which it derived from the Latin word for 'vagina' and which to them meant 'a small sheath' or pod. Orchids were familiar to the Spanish, who were exposed to a specific variety that thrives in the Mediterranean which grew two tubers underground. However, they were unfamiliar with the variety that produced fruit. The Totonacs which they called *xa'nat*, and the Aztecs called it *tlilxochitl* (black pod), which the latter was mistakenly translated by the Spaniards as 'black flower'. Vanilla was used not only as a beverage of consumption, but it was also used as a perfume, incense for the temples of the Aztec gods, and medicine, especially as an antidote for poison.[10]

The uses of vanilla were not recorded at the time of Bernal Díaz del Castillo. The Aztecs guarded the uses of the pods, and the Totonacs did not volunteer much information about them. That is, until Franciscan friar Bernardino de Sahagún arrived in Mexico in 1529 and published *La Historia general de las cosas de Nueva España* (The General History of the Things of New Spain), commonly known as the *Florentine Codex*. Sahagún wrote it in Nahuatl, the Aztecs' own language. He was able to observe and communicate with great detail the customs, religion and everyday life of the Meso-American people. He described a normal remedy made by the indigenous people: 'those who spit blood will get cured drinking cacao made with those aromatic spices called *tlilxochilt* and *ueinacaztli*, as well as with certain kind of pepper called *chiltecpin*, they all well toasted and mixed in with *ulli*.'[11]

The *Florentine Codex* was not published until 264 years after Sahagún's arrival. The first description of the vanilla plant was given by King Philip II's physician and botanist Francisco Hernández de Toledo, who was commissioned by the king to travel to New Spain to study the plants and animals of this new world. He lived in New Spain from 1570 until 1577. During this time, Hernández observed that the indigenous physicians used 'vanilla beans steeped in water to help with urine flow, when adding *mecaxuchit* which is another type of pepper to a chocolate drink it caused abortion . . . vanilla healed female troubles and was good for reducing flatulence'.[12] He ultimately wrote *Rerum medicarum Novae hispaniae thesaurus* (Inventory of Medical Items from New Spain) – a series of six books published in 1607 with descriptions and illustrations of 3,000 plants and their medicinal uses.

An unknown Aztec physician who was baptized as Martin de La Cruz worked on a manuscript of herbal medicine, which

Medicinal writings of Bernardino de Sahagún, from his *Florentine Codex*, livre XI, folio 195.

was translated from Nahuatl to Latin by Juan Badiano. The original title in 1552 was *Libellus de medicinalibus Indorum herbis* (Treatise on Indigenous Medicinal Herbs); however, it was retitled the *Codex de la Cruz-Badiano*. The original manuscript remained in private hands until it was finally published in 1939. Throughout this time, it had several owners, the most notable being the Vatican Library. Pope John Paul II recognized the value of this precious book, which he deemed belonged to the Mexican people. In 1990 it was returned to the Mexican government. It is now part of the National Institute of Anthropology and History's collection.

Europe

The life of the bean continued to evolve from the early seventeenth century in Europe. Charles de l'Écluse, better known as Carolus Clusius, was a botanist and horticulturist. He wrote about the pods after receiving them from Hugh Morgan, apothecary to Queen Elizabeth I. He named the bean *Lobus oblongus aromaticus*, which meant that it was part of a succulent plant species. In 1602, near the end of Elizabeth's reign, Hugh Morgan started using vanilla as a flavouring agent for the monarch's dishes. She wanted all of her food and beverages prepared with these aromatic pods, since she came to believe vanilla was an aphrodisiac, and had a mystical way of improving one's health. Some say that Elizabeth I wanted to improve her sexual prowess, to satisfy her various lovers, though this theory about the Virgin Queen's reign is unproven. As Elizabeth I was the chief influencer of her time, many of her high-born subjects followed suit with her whims of fashion. On top of that, she had an effervescent personality, a lust for life, and a passion to lead her country.

Copy of a lost coronation portrait of Elizabeth I, *c.* 1600.

Élisabeth Louise Vigée Le Brun, *Marie Antoinette in a Chemise Dress*, 1783, oil on canvas.

The eighteenth-century lover and adventurer Giacomo Casanova is famous for his sexual affairs with noble women and anyone he saw to be a good partner, regardless of gender. He was a tall, olive-skinned, curly haired Venetian who could seduce the most cloistered nun. Casanova wrote up his exploits in a memoir called *Histoire de ma vie* (Story of My Life). In his accounts, he records his insatiable appetite for exotic foods. One of his most interesting food orders was when he asked a local baker in the city of Corfu to create a sweet small confection of his lover's lock of hair flavoured with vanilla, angelica and amber.[13]

In 1658 William Piso wrote about how the pods were used by the Spanish. While the use of vanilla as a flavouring agent for chocolate went out of fashion among the Spaniards, the French loved it, and by the eighteenth century they used it more than any other European country to flavour confections and ices.

Louis XIV, king of France, was accustomed to the sweet scent of vanilla. One of his many mistresses, the Marquise de Montespan, bathed in scented waters containing flower petals and vanilla. Louis XVI's legendary wife, Marie Antoinette, had an unquenchable thirst for life. She adored parties and spent excessive amounts of money on luxurious items. She loved perfumes and fell in love with the creations of Jean-Louis Fargeon, who came from a reputable perfumery family. She requested that Jean-Louis create fragrances to fit her every mood. One of her favourites was 'The Secret Garden', made with bergamot, cardamom, jasmine, incense, rose, sandal-wood, vanilla, patchouli, amber and tonka beans.[14]

USA

Vanilla became fashionable in North America after Thomas Jefferson discovered it when serving in Paris as the u.s. ambassador to France from 1785 to 1789. Jefferson lived a life of privilege despite his modest earnings. He took up residence in the Champs-Elysées and placed his daughter in an expensive all-girls school. He also made sure his personal slave, James Hemings, who was of mixed race, was trained in the art of

French cuisine. Thus Hemings became the first American to be trained in French cuisine and pastry arts. Vanilla ice cream is credited to Jefferson, who popularized it, though it was Hemings who actually made the ice cream:

> When Jefferson returned to the United States, he was looking for the pods in the markets of Philadelphia, but there were none to be found. 'Jefferson wrote to William Short, his private secretary while he was living in Paris: He asked Short to send him 50 pods wrapped in the middle of a packet of newspapers.'[15]

As vanilla made it to the North American palate, a rumour started that the best ice cream was made in Philadelphia. Another American who popularized vanilla ice cream was the former First Lady Dolley Madison, wife of James Madison, the fourth president of the United States. Mrs Madison was a charming hostess who served ice cream at her many stately dinners.

Despite such high-profile proponents of vanilla ice cream as these, vanilla's immense popularity in North America did not take off right away due to its scarcity and, as a result, its exorbitant price. The way products were popularized during those times was through home recipes endorsed by homemakers and the manufacturers who published recipe books for their products. But vanilla's bright future was on the horizon. With the demand for the beans came innovation and ingenuity, which would eventually create a more affordable product.

Bass Otis, *Mrs James Madison (Dolley Madison)*, *c.* 1817, oil on canvas.

3
Exporting the Vines

The French and English viewed growing vanilla beans as an exciting new business venture in the making. Vanilla was a luxury item enjoyed only by the European elite. Thus European botanists were studying the plant intensely with a view to local production. As for the Totonac people, the greatest producers of vanilla, they knew the best process for growing it and held this secret back from the Europeans. This ensured that their worth to the Europeans, who enslaved and exterminated indigenous peoples of many of their neighbouring communities, would not be diminished and kept the same fate from befalling them.

Cuttings of vanilla plants were ultimately taken from Mexico with the idea of growing them in Europe and elsewhere. The Europeans had made many failed attempts at growing the vines in tropical areas such as Java, Madagascar and the French colony of Réunion Island (formerly known as Bourbon). Mexico had a two-hundred-year-old monopoly over vanilla exports, which made the beans extremely expensive. Finally, in 1819, the cuttings began to grow successfully on Réunion; however, these plants rarely flowered and never produced any beans.

In 1807, in the gardens of the Right Honourable Charles Greville in Paddington, to the west of London, the first vanilla

Raimundo de Madrazo y Garreta (1841–1920), *Hot Chocolate*, oil on canvas.

vines flowered and some produced fruit. European horticulturists were mystified by the flowering and bean production of the vines. Not until years later was the mystery finally solved.

Professor Charles Morren, a botanist at the University of Liège and member of the Royal Academy of Science in Brussels, conducted several experiments and recorded his observations on paper. Morren made the assertion, on dissecting a vanilla flower, that he could produce vanilla beans of better quality than those from Mexico. After two years of work, in 1836 he discovered that the flowers needed to be individually pollinated in order to produce fruit, and it was the native bees and other animals of Mexico that were responsible for their successful pollination. However, there were no bees outside of Mexico that were able to pollinate them. Morren's discovery enhanced the understanding of what is required to grow the fruit, but his work remained unfinished until Edmond Albius developed a technique for manual pollination years later.

Albius was born a slave in the city of Sainte-Suzanne on Réunion Island in 1829. His mother died giving birth to him. Albius, who had no last name at the time, grew up learning about plants from the owner of the plantation, Féréol Bellier Beaumont.[1] In 1841 Albius found that the vine his master kept alive for 22 years had grown two vanilla beans. Féréol could not understand the occurrence until Albius explained in detail to him how he manually pollinated the vine by opening up the

Engraved portrait of Charles-François-Antoine Morren (1807–1858).

flower and inserting a small stick. Everyone in Réunion was amazed, and Albius became a trainer for all the other plantation slaves on the island, instructing them on the method he used to pollinate the vine. As a token of kindness, Féréol made Albius a free man, for having unlocked the secret of what European horticulturists had been seeking for years. Of course, Albius never saw any monetary profit from his discovery. He died in poverty yet left a legacy that was to be worth millions.

About forty years before this, the naturalist and explorer Alexander von Humboldt began an expedition through Latin America, including Mexico, Central and South America, Cuba and parts of what would become the United States, in an effort to map the botanical geography of the region. Humboldt, born to a wealthy and educated Prussian family in 1769, spared no expense for his mission. His resulting articles, published in *The American Journey*, were revelatory and helped bring vanilla and its production techniques to a wider audience. Not only were scholars, professors and scientific lecturers using his research, but his books and articles exposed amateur biologists and laymen alike to new and exotic species, vanilla included. Humboldt journeyed down the coast of Mexico, then further into Central and South America, describing in great detail – and perhaps for the first time – the vast vanilla production industries that he and his assistants encountered.

Humboldt was particularly impressed with the curing and drying methods he saw being implemented and was awestruck by the amount of vanilla being produced in these areas without the benefit of any kind of man-assisted pollination techniques. Interestingly enough, Humboldt also believed that Spanish cultural bias had hampered the production of vanilla in South America, Venezuela in particular. British and American traders often found poorly stocked inventories of

Curing vanilla beans on a rack.

vanilla in these South American ports. The Spanish, Humboldt observed, considered vanilla to be the cause of various forms of bodily discomfort, including stomach upsets and skin irritation. They therefore avoided adding it to their beloved cacao, causing the market for it to be limited to mostly exports. This would eventually contribute to diminishing vanilla production in Mexico in subsequent decades.

Manufacturing

New developments and advances in science made vanilla more accessible by the late eighteenth century, by which time vanilla had become an important ingredient in sauces, baked goods, beverages and ice cream. In 1847 Joseph Burnett, an American chemist from Boston, developed a method of making vanilla extract. The extract was a pale brown colour, easier to ship and kept better than the whole beans in storage. Vanillin, the dominant flavour component of the cured beans, was isolated in 1858 by the French biochemist Nicolas-Théodore Gobley, who crystallized it from vanilla extract. In 1874 the German scientists Ferdinand Tiemann and Wilhelm Haarmann developed a way to synthesize vanillin by using coniferin, a component of pine bark. In 1891 the French chemist De Taire extracted vanillin from eugenol, an aromatic liquid extracted from clove oil. Another way of making synthetic vanillin is from coal, tar or sulphite liquid, a by-product of wood pulp that is typically used to make paper. After the synthetic flavour was developed, it enabled vanilla products to be manufactured commercially, and this in turn gave vanilla the opportunity to complete its conquest of our senses and palates.

Between 1886 and 1897, the soft drink and ice cream industries would introduce several products to consumers that would cause the demand for vanilla to skyrocket. Because of the declining price of sugar, confectionery producers had already begun flooding the market with chocolates of all shapes, sizes and qualities. Yet it would be two other, very similar industries that would eventually dominate vanilla usage, far surpassing that of the confectionery, fragrance and pharmaceutical industries.

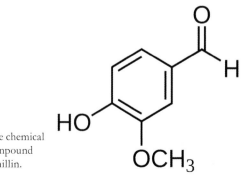

The chemical compound vanillin.

Ice cream preceded soft drinks in the United States by more than one hundred years, but it wasn't until the mid-1800s, just a few decades before the arrival of Coca-Cola, that it became the sensation we know it as today. In 1747 the first recipe appeared in a book by Hannah Glasse, an English housewife and later a dressmaker for the royals. She wrote *The Art of Cookery*, which instructs housewives to add vanilla to chocolate.[2] Mary Randolph, an American housewife, published *The Virginia Housewife* cookbook, and included the first North American ice cream recipe in 1824.[3]

Again, it was the advent of artificial vanilla pollination that helped create the craze for the cold, sweetened treats. Vanilla became more affordable than ever, and thus quickly became the most popular flavour of ice cream.

After ice cream, soft drinks rose in popularity, and initially one of their most notable uses was as a medicinal tonic, with vanilla as part of the recipe. This was not a novelty, though. Meso-American civilizations had used vanilla with their herbal remedies, a legacy that survived for many centuries. Vanilla was prescribed by doctors for various afflictions until 1910, when it was deemed unsafe for human consumption.

Dr John Stith Pemberton, a pharmacist and a former soldier, was addicted to morphine, which he needed to relieve him from a painful wound he had obtained in the Battle of Columbus in 1865. He first invented 'Dr Tuggle's Compound Syrup of Globe Flower' as his pain medication replacement for morphine.[4] However, the ingredients were toxic and he came up with a better and safer alternative called 'Pemberton's French Wine Coca'. In 1886 he refined the recipe and called it cola syrup.

Imitation carbonated water was invented in 1767 by Joseph Priestley in Leeds, England. In 1810 the innovators Simmons and Rundell of South Carolina obtained the patent to mass-produce soda water.[5] Between 1859 and 1883, the soda fountain concept evolved, serving mixtures of carbonated water and flavoured syrup. In 1886 John Pemberton began selling cups of cola mixed with carbonated water for a nickel at his friend's drugstore. Pemberton's friend and personal accountant, Frank Robinson, brainstormed the idea of this cola mixture and named it Coca-Cola.[6] It was an immediate sensation, grabbing the attention of Asa Griggs Candler, a business tycoon with a flair for marketing. While Pemberton's mixture was centred on the medicinal benefits of Coca-Cola, Candler was more savvy and suspected that the sweet flavour profile of the drink would be its selling point. Sure enough, after Pemberton sold the rights of his company to Candler in 1888, shortly before he died, his sugary concoction began to dominate the market. Candler's first move was to expand the business by selling the Coca-Cola syrup to wholesalers, who then sold it to drugstores.

The success of Coca-Cola inspired competitors to use the alluring sweetness of vanilla to come up with similar flavoured syrups and carbonated drinks, all touting unique and wonderful tastes. Dr Pepper was introduced in 1885 and proved almost as popular as Coca-Cola. About ten years after that, Pepsi-Cola came on to the scene and began an epic battle with Coca-Cola for soft drink supremacy that continues to this day. The expanded selection and growing variety of sodas were served at soda fountains and ice cream parlours, which were quite popular at that time, as well as in local pharmacies and drugstores.

Vanilla-flavoured syrup was added to nearly all of these beverages before being served to customers. Among the most popular drinks in the soda fountains were floats, which contained vanilla ice cream and flavoured carbonated soda. There were also various 'Cow' drinks with different flavours. The

Advertisement for Coca-Cola, c. 1890s.

Brown Cow included vanilla ice cream, chocolate syrup and cola carbonated water, while the Black Cow had root beer as its base, vanilla ice cream, carbonated water and no chocolate syrup.

What accounted for the success of the soft drink industry? Besides the fact that the sweet, sugary and altogether

Women and men at a soda fountain, early 20th century.

pleasant-tasting beverage practically sold itself, other external factors played a large role. The discovery of artificial vanilla pollination enabled production to increase enormously and aided in the development of the vanilla extract and imitations of the real flavour. Vanilla plantations on a massive scale were developed throughout Latin America, Mexico, the Caribbean and the far-flung islands in the Indian Ocean. As production increased to meet demand, prices fell dramatically, and vanilla, formerly an out-of-reach product enjoyed by the affluent and wealthy, became obtainable by nearly anyone with a few cents in their pockets for a soda pop.

Americans' love affair with vanilla came not only with ice cream and pastries, but with chocolate confectionery as well, thanks to advances in manufacturing and manual pollination. The Europeans, especially the Swiss and Belgians, were renowned for chocolates made with vanilla. Milton Hershey, a philanthropic capitalist, built a factory in 1905 in what was to become known as Hershey, in Derry Township, Pennsylvania. Hershey was determined to compete with the European chocolate manufacturing market and did so on a global scale. Thus Hershey's Kisses were born, and became – and remain – one of the factory's signature products. The ingredients are milk chocolate (sugar, milk, chocolate, cocoa butter, lactose, milk fat, soy lecithin, glycerol and fatty acids, which come from castor beans or soy oil), emulsifiers and vanillin. To this day, Hershey is still manufacturing chocolate products and has successfully switched to natural vanilla in its formulas.

4
The Modern World

Prior to the Second World War, vanilla importation and usage was in a state of flux, caused primarily by enforcement of the Prohibition Act until 1935 and by the Great Depression that began in the United States in 1929 and soon spread across the globe. Production and shipping disruptions caused by extreme weather events and labour instability added to these challenges.

Ocean shipping lanes, crucial to exporting and importing every type of merchandise, became difficult to navigate even before the war began. As soon as it escalated, these shipping lanes were closed to non-military vessels. First, lane closures in and around the Indian Ocean halted shipments to Europe, while American-assisted Tahitian production ground to a halt as well. Not long thereafter, Axis and Allied warships began swarming the Atlantic Ocean, which made shipments along those lines equally treacherous. The United States was forced to rely on Mexico and the Caribbean islands for vanilla, boosting their struggling industries.

As it was, vanilla usage in America was thwarted by wartime rationing, which created shortages of nearly every kind of meat, poultry and dairy product imaginable. These precious items were being sent overseas to feed the country's fighting forces. Women were recruited to replace men in the domestic workforce, and those former homemakers now had neither the luxury nor time to bake and cook. The limited amount of natural vanilla that eventually found its way into the U.S. was monopolized by several large industrial pastry companies and the growing ice cream industry. Yet even that diminished as the war progressed.

Two fascinating incidents occurred during this period that not only confirmed vanilla's growing appeal, but pointed to a future in which it would become ingrained in the USA's collective culture and psyche. The U.S. Navy, under pressure from powerful politicians in Washington, DC (along with thousands of vanilla- and chocolate-starved sailors), created a 'floating ice cream' production facility that could produce up to 9,000 litres (2,000 gallons) a day and transported it throughout the Pacific in an effort to increase morale.[1] Smaller-scale factories were established by the U.S. Army near the front lines of Europe.

Hostess Brands, a rapidly growing manufacturer of packaged cakes and pastries, was caught in a quandary. Bananas, which Hostess had used to fill its light and airy (and profitable) sponge cakes since purchasing the brand from the Continental Baking Company several years earlier, were also in very short supply because of wartime rationing.[2] After several other fruit-flavoured variations were produced and tested, with mixed success, Hostess settled on a vanilla-flavoured Twinkie. It was not an entirely popular choice within the company. Many Hostess executives feared that vanilla was too insipid and boring a flavour to replace the original banana Twinkie. Others felt that reliance on the more readily available synthetic vanillin could compromise the quality and reputation of the product. Indeed, the company's sceptics were expressing a prejudice against the flavour that would only spread and deepen in the coming decades. Nevertheless,

Second World War poster of Rosie the Riveter created to recruit women to enter the workforce: 'We Can Do It!'

this new vanilla Twinkie was an immediate sensation and continues to be made today. Hostess began incorporating more vanilla into its other popular brands as well. Around seventy years later, Hostess Brands would file for bankruptcy protection twice, in 2004 and 2012, halt production and deprive fans of the legendary Twinkie. This in turn led to stockpiling by American consumers who were afraid of the lack of Twinkies available to them, until production resumed the following year.[3]

When the war finally concluded in 1945, hundreds of thousands of men and women returned home to the United States. Many of them had been away for years and found themselves in a country in the midst of massive economic and social change. As the men went back to work, the women, who had joined the workforce to take the place of the deployed men, were asked to resume their former lives as homemakers. Food manufacturers, and particularly Madison Avenue, were well aware of this cultural sea change and were ready to take advantage. Soon, a mind-boggling assortment of food products became readily available to housewives throughout the country. Products such as canned vegetables and TV dinners promised nutrition, flavour and, above all, simplicity and efficiency.

But in this prosperous and bustling new era, it was cake, confectionery, ice cream, pudding and other reassuring desserts that consumers craved, perhaps to help them forget about the recent past and prepare for a hopefully more affluent and happy future. Moist and spongy chiffon and angel food cakes were ubiquitous and all the rage, but it was the popularity of processed and boxed cake, pudding and Jell-O mixes that really took off and pointed the way to how desserts would be prepared and served in the coming years. The Pillsbury, Duncan Hines and Jell-O brands, which still dominate dessert aisles in American supermarkets today, offered up a vast array of sweet options while introducing new products on what seemed a daily basis.

The explosion of vanilla-infused products was helped along by the now widespread use of commercial and domestic refrigeration methods. This made it possible to efficiently manufacture and transport frozen goods to shops and supermarkets and, ultimately, to household refrigerators. As difficult as it is to believe, it was not until the late 1940s that the first mass-produced ice cream products began to see nationwide distribution. Frozen cakes of all varieties would also fill the refrigerators of various marketplaces. And vanilla-flavoured dairy products such as yoghurt gained popularity as advances in cooling and transportation improved.

The birth and proliferation of supermarkets and other self-service shops were instrumental in making the procurement of food items affordable and simple, and their impact on daily life in the U.S. and Europe cannot be overestimated. While the concept of supermarkets gained traction in the 1930s, it wasn't until two decades later that they began to dominate and push out smaller food shops and markets. The rise in automobile usage and the onset of suburban sprawl contributed enormously to this change, as well. These modifications in shopping habits, largely viewed as positive developments for consumers, have greatly impacted the success of smaller food sellers and suppliers. Supermarkets have also attracted harsh criticism for the large amounts of food items that expire before purchase, including perishable vanilla items.

The rapid growth and propagation of fast-food restaurants and diners also fed the growing demand for vanilla. The potent combination of a booming post-war economy and larger families was effectively exploited by the food and service industries, which answered the challenge by greatly increasing the number of fast-food restaurants while simultaneously rolling out a wide variety of so called 'family-style' restaurants. My husband and I have often recalled wonderful and evocative shared memories of thick, ice-cold vanilla milkshakes from McDonald's on hot summer nights, or pulling off the New Jersey Turnpike or the Garden State Parkway and entering the Howard Johnson car park, anticipating the wonderful taste of their restaurant's incredible vanilla ice cream sodas.

Most Americans became more prosperous during the post-war years, and the staggering amount of food ingredients available to the average housewife could often make cooking decisions confusing and nerve-wracking. The publishing industry, always looking to take advantage of new trends, began releasing cookbooks aimed at harried women who needed to cook for several growing children and a husband on his way home from work. Good Housekeeping, Betty Crocker and Birds Eye frozen foods (not affiliated with Birdseye publishing company) led the way, with dozens of smaller publishing houses adding to the variety. Most of these mass-produced books contained very conventional and conservative recipes that used supermarket staples, although some would expose food preparers to exotic flavours and ingredients that were already slowly making inroads into

Vanilla cupcakes with frosting.

Cover of *Betty Crocker's Cook Book for Boys and Girls* (1957), illustrated by Gloria Kamen.

American stores and households. Some would go on to have a profound impact on food preparation for decades to come, such as Julia Child's *Mastering the Art of French Cooking*, published in 1961 with the assistance of the French cooks Louisette Bertholle and Simone Beck. Child's *The French Chef*, one of the first televised cooking programmes, would also prove instrumental in the growth of unique and diverse food preparation methods.

Whether it was because of the concerns of newly conscientious consumers or in order to protect the integrity of their products, quality maintenance was high on the agendas of vanilla and vanilla-extract makers during the 1950s and '6os. Imitation and synthetic vanillas and extracts had, because of the scarcity and the prohibitive costs of natural vanilla, gained traction during the previous thirty years. Lax label laws meant that producers could describe their products in any way they wished, often advertising inferior products as 'natural' or 'pure'. At the time, vanilla-testing facilities were practically non-existent. Standards for vanilla integrity were sorely needed.

Perhaps not surprisingly, it was the industry's undisputed leader and the largest flavour company in the u.s., McCormick & Company, which pushed hardest for regulation. Many of McCormick's competitors opposed new labelling standards because they felt these would only be to McCormick's benefit. Some of the competitors resisted regulation just to spite them. The established Flavor and Extract Manufacturers Association was primarily concerned with the production, shipping and legal aspects of the industry, but it wasn't responsible for monitoring the quality or veracity of vanilla products. That was left to the Food and Drug Administration (FDA). After a decade-long, much contested legal battle, the FDA finally issued industry-backed standards in 1962.

These newly enforced vanilla standards, and most other food and beverage labelling standards, were in the service of the ingredients often found in processed foods. These processed foods, while sometimes being healthy, more often than not contained added salt, sugar and fat, while actually containing less nutritional density. This practice continues to this day and is often cited as contributing to various health issues, such as obesity. Yet the trend towards a healthy diet and exercise lifestyle, which began in the 1960s and gained more exposure and acceptance during the 1970s, would have yet another profound effect on the vanilla industry.

During a time when buzzwords and concepts such as 'organic', 'locally sourced' and 'back to nature' have become ubiquitous to the point of becoming cliché, it can be difficult to imagine an era when such concerns were held by only a small group of people, typically those thought to be on the fringe. These prescient youngsters and professionals were often derided as 'hippies' and 'tree huggers'. What they lacked in numbers, however, they more than made up for in determination and righteousness.

This movement began in earnest when a small number of baby boomers, those who were born just after the end of the Second World War, decided to turn their backs on what they believed to be a hectic, stressful capitalistic rat race. They elected to espouse a simpler life, one that included home-grown, organic and natural foods. They were also vocal advocates of protecting the environment from the encroachment of corporate and capitalist greed. Although they were mocked at first, their ideology gained traction and, helped along substantially and somewhat cynically by corporate interests and Madison Avenue marketing, ultimately became a fully fledged movement in the early 2000s.

As this movement began to build some steam, cafés, markets and restaurants specializing in healthy eating began opening and marketed themselves as a substitute for the substantially less healthy fast-food and family-style restaurants. (This growth remained slow until the advent in the 1980s of larger, supermarket-style stores like Whole Foods that catered to those looking for organic and healthy alternatives.) At first, these were primarily located in large, coastal cities such as New York City and the Bay Area on the West Coast, where consumers were inclined to be educated and well-to-do, as organics tend to be costlier. They soon spread to college towns, exposing young adults to a new way of enjoying food. These newfangled restaurants would often produce ice cream, cookies and cakes using organic or low-fat ingredients to entice customers into their establishments, with costly all-natural vanilla being a featured component.

The 1980s and '90s marked a prosperous period in the United States and much of the rest of the world. An increasingly educated, wealthy and open-minded population demanded more exotic foods and experiences. After a lull in the 1980s, trends in healthy and organic foods and dining options began to form once more. The media, particularly the television and publishing industries, jumped on the bandwagon, producing an incredible quantity of food and dining content. Cookbooks, largely relegated to your mother's cluttered kitchen drawer or to bookshop bargain bins, exploded

Vanilla cream cheese pie.

in popularity. Television and cable stations were suddenly awash with programmes featuring the newest media darlings – celebrity chefs. Yet it was in the rapidly expanding health and experience industries that the use of vanilla, more than ever before, regained its ability to captivate and, yes, even titillate the population.

While organic and healthy foods were gaining market share, processed foods high in sugar and fat content still dominated supermarket shelves and filled America's food pantries. Owing to faster-paced lifestyles and less time spent consuming carefully prepared meals, obesity levels saw a steep rise. Low-fat and fat-free options, which had been nothing more than niche products in the past, gained widespread acceptance and soon filled supermarket and grocery store shelves. New, beautifully packaged and presented 'healthy' products would come to market, with TV and print advertisements celebrating their ability to trim your waistline. Of course, most of these items contained large quantities of salt and sugar, negating any supposed health benefits.

Manufacturers of 'diet' products also had to deal with an unfortunate reality: food and beverages made with lower levels of fat or sugars tended to be bland and tasteless, and what flavour remained was often bitter and metallic. Enter vanilla, which producers procured and used in many of these items to mask such unpleasant tastes, increase flavour and improve mouth feel. Vanilla would go on to augment not only standbys such as cookies, cakes and ice cream, but newer products as well. Breakfast shakes, athletic protein drinks and yoghurts became extremely popular and featured vanilla as their primary flavour enhancer.

At the same time, self-improvement and self-help methods and trends came into vogue in the 1960s and '70s. Previously ridiculed by the media and researchers alike, these approaches to self-esteem and self-help gained increased acceptance in the 1980s and '90s, as newly conducted studies ascribed multiple benefits to them. These practices often promoted a slower, less stressful lifestyle. To that effect, aromatherapy began to be used to complement stress-reducing activities such as meditation, yoga and low-impact strength conditioning.

Patricia Rain, in *Vanilla: The Cultural History of the World's Most Popular Flavor and Fragrance*, cites an aromatherapy study conducted by Sloan-Kettering in New York City which found that vanilla, a homey scent which may remind people of food, was well received. Recently, the commercial popularity of vanilla fragrance has risen accordingly.[4] The ever-growing list of products utilizing vanilla included not only fine perfumes, but air fresheners, potpourri, candles and various types of skincare products. Unconfirmed reports even suggested that it was used in recently manufactured automobiles to give them their 'new car' scent. Similar studies, such as those conducted by psychiatrist Alan Hirsch, neurological director of the Smell and Taste Treatment and Research Foundation in Chicago, also appear to confirm what had been believed for centuries: that there is a clear link between the scent of vanilla and sexual desire, arousal and even performance. Naturally, these studies were exploited to market products such as perfumes and colognes, a strategy which found considerable success.

With its incredible versatility and allure, it is no surprise that producers and consumers alike continue to find unique and interesting uses for vanilla. History shows us that even seemingly innocuous and taken-for-granted items can ingrain themselves in our culture and our everyday lives. In the case of vanilla, this was no mere quirk or accident. Many talented and creative people struggled mightily over the decades to ensure the popularity and availability of this

Candles, flowers and spices for aromatherapy.

magnificent product. These same people, as well as those who simply treasure vanilla, look to the future, where the possibilities and potential appear endless.

5
Supply and Production

During the twentieth century, trends, fads and cultures all confirmed the appeal and versatility of vanilla, and thus the demand for it skyrocketed. Successful vanilla cultivation and production on the island of Réunion after 1841 showed unequivocally that the development of a vanilla industry could be both profitable and successful elsewhere. With the proper conditions, a fair amount of patience, and a tremendous amount of effort, vanilla could yield an enormous financial windfall to those prepared to produce and supply it. In rapid succession, other regional islands such as the Seychelles and Mauritius began emulating Réunion's methods, scoring successes of their own. Many of these neophyte growers came to believe that vanilla was the superior cash crop to mainstays such as sugar and fruit. Exporters on these islands had little difficulty selling their valuable vanilla to willing and demanding importers and sellers throughout Western Europe.

Other island nations such as Indonesia and Tahiti, where vanilla production struggled or wasn't encouraged, entered the market in the early years of the twentieth century. And, as the incentives to grow vanilla became clearer, countries throughout the world, on several continents, began their own vanilla industries. Nations as disparate as China, Uganda and even the United States took notice of the growing demand for, and consistent popularity and widespread use of, vanilla and would eventually jump into the fray on the supply side.

Sri Lanka, Comoros, Madagascar, Seychelles and other countries in the Indian Ocean increased the size and scope of their existing production facilities while opening new ones on neighbouring islands. Indonesia ramped up production. The prospect of complete success, however, fell victim to the major storms that rocked the largest suppliers of vanilla in the Indian Ocean region, mainly Indonesia and Madagascar.

Therefore, vanilla production was cut in half, causing prices to swell to $46 per kilogram in 2000, compared to $16.25 in 1999. Vanilla prices have fluctuated in the last few decades. In Mexico, production was hindered by poor land usage and maintenance. Mexico's government had favoured the burgeoning crude oil and livestock industries over the previous few decades, and they even levelled a large amount of their existing rainforests to make way for cattle farms and oil rigs.

The biggest vanilla producer by far is Madagascar. The trends there, as in other growing regions, are quite unsettling. Climate change, criminal enterprise, the lack of development and price escalation continue to plague the industry. Madagascar has been hit by several major cyclones, the last one being Cyclone Enawo in 2017, its strongest storm to make landfall since 2004. This was followed by severe drought, creating serious vanilla shortages. This is difficult enough for importers and those who use the product, but for the farmers who toil to bring vanilla to market, it can be ruinous. These farmers receive as little as 5 to 10 per cent of the value for their crops, so when sharp price increases occur, or when consumers seek synthetics as an alternative to natural vanilla, their livelihoods are negatively impacted. Food insecurity is quite common during these periods, as is resorting to crime to make ends meet.

Sacks full of vanilla pods ready to be transported by porters, Madagascar.

Crime, in fact, has become an increasingly worrisome issue in recent years. The theft of valuable maturing beans right from the vine is a very common occurrence. Even green beans will fetch a fairly decent price on the market. Calls have been made for government-sponsored armed police units, while vigilante groups have captured and killed numerous bean thieves. Farmers, desperate to protect their vanilla, counter theft by bringing in their crops early. Consequently, the market becomes flooded with poor-quality beans, and when quality drops, typically so do prices. Also, a flourishing yet highly illegal rosewood trade worth hundreds of millions of dollars per year has sprung up in the region, whereby the wood is sold to China and other Southeast Asian countries. Profits are then laundered by purchasing vanilla at reduced prices.

Similar complications have occurred in other major growing locations, such as Indonesia, Mexico and China, the last of which now ranks third of all vanilla-producing nations. China has also had to deal with increasing wage demands from its workers – demands which may stall production there – but the country has been known to assist other emerging vanilla producers such as Uganda. With an annual vanilla yield that remains second only to Madagascar, Indonesia has had to deal with massive flooding caused by deforestation and other questionable land usage policies.

Vanilla buyers cannot and will not continue to pay exorbitant prices for pure vanilla, whether it's grown and produced in Madagascar, Indonesia, Mexico or China. The demand for pure vanilla has decreased substantially, and steeper prices may sharpen this trend. Furthermore, industrial artificial curing and synthetic vanillas are being progressively accepted as substitutes in restaurants, supermarkets and households. Tens of thousands of vanilla growers who use traditional hand-curing methods may find their livelihood threatened by inflated prices.

The use of synthetic vanillin, which has become more widespread over the years, has gained further traction in industries that relied on pure vanilla. Advances in technology made synthetics much more palatable to both businesses and consumers. When vanilla production and prices eventually stabilized, many businesses, for obvious fiscal reasons, chose to continue to utilize synthetics in their products, causing further market instability that lasted for a decade.

Yet recent positive developments, both locally and abroad, offer hope to a beleaguered industry. Consumers worldwide, and particularly in the United States, are demanding healthy and all-natural ingredients in their food and beverages and are increasingly conscious of how these ingredients are grown and brought to market. Food and flavouring companies, ever aware of consumer trends, had been reformulating their products for years in an effort to claim 'organic' or 'all-natural' ingredients on labels and in advertising. This movement was fortified when Nestlé proclaimed that they would be eliminating all artificial additives to their chocolate products, necessitating increased imports of vanilla since they had been primarily using synthetic vanillin to improve the flavour of their chocolate. Hershey's, General Mills, Kellogg's and others soon followed suit.

Consumers and, ultimately, the companies who cater to them are also increasingly concerned about how their food and beverages are sourced and the extent to which farmers and labourers benefit from their toils. A growing and quite vocal assortment of consumers and buyers are insisting on fair trade agreements. Fair trade, defined as 'trade between companies in developed countries and producers in developing countries in which fair prices are paid to the producers', also addresses such hot-topic subjects as improved social standards for growers, as well as various environmental concerns. Many fair trade organizations, such as the Livelihood Fund, educate farmers on sustainable practices and organize vanilla protection groups to combat theft. While fair trade has been very effective in other industries like coffee and chocolate, it has been, thus far, less successful for vanilla growers. Fair trade organizations ask for a fee to inspect and certify vanilla, a cost many growers cannot afford. Weather conditions and changing climates continue to add volatility to the industry and make fair trade difficult to implement and much harder to enforce.

While the future of vanilla production remains somewhat uncertain and full of questions, it nevertheless holds a great deal of promise. Despite the persistent encroachment of synthetic vanillas, the vanilla industry, as a whole, should continue to benefit enormously from shifts in consumer preferences as people seek 'the real thing' and weigh social and environmental concerns. Continued production disruptions in Madagascar have opened the door to an amazing array of production facilities throughout the world, offering an incredible assortment of vanilla commodities, yet they need to resist the impulse to make quick profits by resorting to, for example, early harvesting and smuggling. By favouring long-term opportunity over short-term windfalls, and building a reputation for quality, established and emerging producers alike have the potential to ensure vanilla's availability and popularity. That, along with its versatility, appealing and exotic aroma and flavour profile, and surprisingly complex backstory, should ensure vanilla's position in the marketplace, as well as its place in people's hearts, for decades to come.

World Trade

Leading Importers of Vanilla Beans, 2017[1]

RANK	COUNTRY	PERCENTAGE	IMPORT VALUE $
1	United States	43	575,000,000
2	France	20	271,000,000
3	Germany	10	137,000,000
4	Mauritius	3.9	52,000,000
5	Netherlands	3.1	41,400,000
6	Japan	3.1	41,200,000
7	India	2.5	33,500,000
8	Switzerland	2.0	27,000,000
9	Italy	1.2	16,400,000
10	United Kingdom	1.2	15,500,000

Leading Countries Producing Vanilla Beans, 2016[2]

RANK	COUNTRY	TONS OF VANILLA PRODUCED
1	Madagascar	2,926
2	Indonesia	2,304
3	China	885
4	Mexico	513
5	Papua New Guinea	502
6	Turkey	303
7	Uganda	211
8	Tonga	180
9	French Polynesia	24
10	Réunion	21
11	Malawi	20
12	Comoros	15
13	Kenya	15
14	Guadeloupe	11
15	Zimbabwe	11

Total world production of bean varieties

V. planifolia	97 per cent
V. tahitensis	2 per cent
V. pompona	1 per cent

Price of first-grade vanilla, 2019

1 kg (2.2 lb)	$500

6
Pop Culture

Open up a blank Microsoft Word document, and type the word 'vanilla', then right click and select 'synonyms'. What alternative word options are listed?

Plain. Bland. Boring. Ordinary. The list drones on. Yet how has something that has boasted such a rich, fascinating and tumultuous history become synonymous with blandness? How can something possessing as enticing a fragrance and flavour profile as vanilla obtain such a status as ordinary when it is anything but?

Vanilla was once a very rare commodity. It was obtained for, and used exclusively by, the wealthy. By the 1950s, vanilla was everywhere, used in almost everything and easily obtainable. In recent decades, it has become overused to the point of ubiquity. Soft drinks, cookies, cakes, yoghurt – just about anything that is baked or sweetened contains vanilla. The origins of plain, unembellished items being classified as 'vanilla' can probably be traced back to the engineering and electrical industries that arose during the post-Second World War economic boom, though it was the information technology industries that began in the 1970s that were most instrumental in adding vanilla-as-plain to the American language. To this day, when a computer or laptop is unboxed for the first time, its operating system, or image, is described as vanilla, meaning that it is totally unadorned and without the added software and applications that will make it more useful.

In 1971 the Pittsburgh-based independent film-maker George Romero's *There's Always Vanilla* was released in several movie cinemas throughout the USA, and then seemed to disappear as quickly as it had arrived. Romero was riding high off his success with the 1968 low-budget shocker *Night of the Living Dead* and, in an effort not to be typecast as merely another horror film director, chose this unassuming and rather uncommercial project as his follow-up. With much of *Night of the Living Dead*'s production crew and a minuscule $70,000 budget, production commenced on what would ultimately become a rather sloppy and uninspired romantic comedy. Yet the film remains interesting as an early example of vanilla being used as a somewhat unflattering adjective. Towards the end of the film, the main character's father, while dining at a Howard Johnson's, explains to him that 'life is like an ice cream parlor, and that of all of life's most exotic flavors to choose from, there's always vanilla to fall back on.'

In a world with an almost unlimited variety of flavours and scents, and with new and exciting ones introduced on what seems like a daily basis, vanilla is now considered plain and boring, as something which lacks other flavours. Or, it is viewed as a safe choice when confronted with numerous flavour options. As the vanilla-as-plain meme has become ingrained in our collective psyche, so too has it made its way into popular culture, and nowhere more so than in the music industry.

What do the recording artists Abba, the Carpenters, Doris Day, Olivia Newton-John and Pat Boone have in common? They differ in terms of their nationalities, genders and musical genres, but what they all share is the dubious distinction of having themselves – or their music – labelled as 'vanilla'.

Collectively, the songs and sounds that they have produced over the years have been formally branded as vanilla pop.

Vanilla pop typically, if not always, features similar traits: expensive, crystal-clear studio recording, otherworldly sound effects used to add gloss to a simple, unadorned vocal delivery and/or unassuming song structure. Besides being carefully constructed, vanilla pop also tends to be unthreatening and unassertive. The songs avoid any striving for authenticity, and there is certainly no room for 'street cred' – two labels favoured, and desperately sought after, by vanilla pop's more boisterous relatives, rock and jazz music.[1] Yet, what some listeners consider turn-offs, others consider to be strengths. In an increasingly coarse, loud and ostentatious time, vanilla pop's offerings of syrupy, safe and lightweight melodies continue to give respite to those in need of it, and this bodes well for the genre's rediscovery, if not its popularity.

The following are examples of vanilla pop from the late 1950s to 1990:

'sos', 'The Name of the Game', and 'Dancing
    Queen' by Abba
'Rainy Days and Mondays' by the Carpenters
The Best of Bread (the entire album) by Bread
'The Things We Did Last Summer' by the Four
    Preps
'Blue Velvet' by Bobby Vinton

In 1989, 22-year-old Robert Matthew Van Winkle released a cover of Wild Cherry's pop-funk classic 'Play That Funky Music'. The reception that it received from both radio programmers and the listening public was underwhelming, to say the least. Van Winkle, recording and performing under the moniker Vanilla Ice, was quite disappointed by its performance in the clubs and on the charts. That was, until DJs began spinning the song's B-side, a catchy little tune with a memorable bass line entitled 'Ice, Ice Baby'. The song exploded and soon became the first hip-hop single to top the Billboard Hot 100 list. The impact of the song on that era's pop culture was extraordinary.

Equally extraordinary, however, was the intense backlash spawned by the song's incredible success. Ice, who had acquired his nickname years earlier because he was the only white member of a collection of breakdancing and rapping friends, would soon be accused of being a phoney and a fraud. Plagiarism accusations swirled. More troubling, he was also accused of cultural misappropriation.[2] His adoption of African American elements into his music and persona was harshly criticized. He was denounced for living up to his name. He and his music are now scathingly and mockingly described as being vanilla.

Nearly thirty years later, as Ice prepared to take part in the upcoming 'I Love the '90s' tour, he was asked about the state of modern music. He enthusiastically described it as dull, uninteresting and unable to stand the test of time. In essence, he was accusing it of being vanilla.

As Vanilla Ice can attest, the word 'vanilla' can be used as much more than just an adjective. The term is now often used to describe being Caucasian. The implications of this logic go far beyond the focus and scope of this book, but as a perusal of university and college curriculum options and opinion/editorial sections in major newspapers and websites on any given day illustrates, there is no shortage of views on these controversial subjects.

Vanilla has invaded our language in myriad ways. 'Vanilla sex' is sex that does not include erotic elements. In other words, it's just ordinary sex, missionary style. When someone labels you as 'too vanilla', it means that you are boring or not interesting. How could such an erotic flavour have become boring? We have been desensitized to its once controversial taste by placing it everywhere, using it in everything. And while vanilla has become a staple part of the culture, it is no longer viewed as a special added spice, but a mainstay in all aspects of our lives.

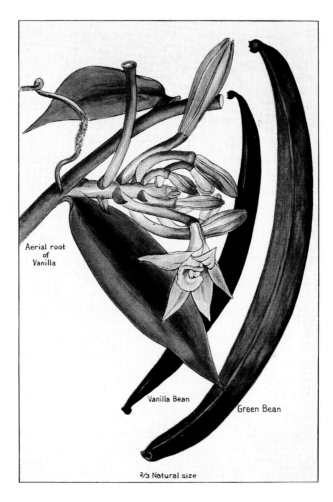

Aerial root
of
Vanilla

Vanilla Bean

Green Bean

2/3 Natural size

McCormick & Company drawing of vanilla plants, flowers
and beans, 1915.

7
Flavour Profile

Vanilla's enticing aroma has most likely been its primary selling point and focus of its appeal since the Meso-Americans first picked it up from the forest grounds and realized that it was much more than a shrivelled black stick. Modern-day chemists and perfumers describe its aroma as 'earthy and woodsy, floral, hay-like, rummy, smoky, sweet, spicy, tobacco-like, with hints of everything from prunes and raisins to almonds, bananas and even cotton candy'.[1] As we have previously learned, vanilla's primary flavour, vanillin, is found in other sources such as 'whisky, rum, white and red wine, the juice of barley, sugar cane and grape juice which has been fermented in oak barrels'.[2]

Vanillin

Vanillin has between 250 and 500 organic components. The orchid is not the only plant that produces vanillin. 'The Ponderosa, Jeffrey and Red Chinese pine trees produce vanillin, as do Firs and sapwood. Vanillin is detected when cellulose fibers are separated from the trees while it is being converted to pulp, which is eventually used for paper products.'[3] Another orchid variety, *Leptotes bicolor*, found primarily in Paraguay

Ponderosa pine tree on the Tronsen Ridge Trail.

and south Brazil, also contains vanillin and can be used as a vanilla substitute.

Other notable plants that offer a vanilla-like essence include deertongue, found in coastal regions of the u.s. between North Carolina and Florida, which was once used by Native Americans to scent the air, and the vanilla leaf, also known as the sweet after death, found in the u.s. Pacific Northwest. The latter is typically used to repel insects. 'Tonka beans, grown in the forests of Brazil and British Guiana, contain high levels of a chemical compound called Coumadin.'[4] These beans had been used in the past as a vanilla extract substitute due to their sweet flavour. However, research has shown 'that Coumadin is toxic to the liver when consumed in large quantities and [it] is now banned in the u.s. by the Food and Drug Administration'.[5] Sweet clover, a bitter herb formerly imported from Europe into the United States, contains Coumadin as well. In Mexico, tourists and international travellers will often come across inexpensive bottles of vanilla sold in outdoor markets. At times, these cheap vanilla knockoffs contain a significant amount of Coumadin.

Industrial manufacturers currently produce nearly 15,000 tons of synthesized vanillin annually using a substance called 'guaiacol, a component found in clove oil, wood pulp and petroleum by-products. *Castereoum*, an even more expensive substitute, is created by using secretions from the anal glands and castor sacs of beavers,'[6] which the mammals produce and use to mark their territory. This extract has a warm, sweet aroma and is often used as a substitute for vanilla extract in dairy products and baked goods. It had been widely used by the perfume industry until this practice was halted because of concerns over the inhumane treatment of the beavers during the hunting, trapping and collection processes.

Consequently, businesses that rely on vanilla and its distinctive natural flavour and aroma for their products will often, because of high costs, resort to using artificial or synthetic flavouring instead of pure vanilla. Because of unpredictable and harsh weather conditions, political circumstances and difficult and time-consuming cultivation practices, the price of vanilla has increased far above the rate of inflation in vanilla-producing countries like Madagascar. And because of crop failure and the occasional bust market, its availability is not always reliable or guaranteed. Despite the advantages of their wide availability and low cost, synthetics are far inferior to the complexity and flavour of pure vanilla.

Extracts

The highest-quality extracts will have a rich perfumed fragrance, be amber in colour and low in sugar. Also, some extracts are labelled 'Bourbon', which simply means that the beans used in the extract came from either Madagascar, the Comoro Islands or Réunion Island. When you buy vanilla extract, close the lid tightly and store the bottle in a cool, dark place. If you expose it to heat and light, it loses its potency.

The most important thing is to look for 'pure vanilla extract' on the label. The contents are water, alcohol (minimum 35 per cent), and 13.5 per cent of vanilla bean extractions per gallon, according to the FDA. The extract contains sugar, colouring or preservatives, and this must be printed on the label. When more sugar is added to the extract, it helps the extract mature faster, making the flavour more subtle. Other extracts contain caramelized sugar, giving them a dark and muddy appearance. Organic premium vanilla extracts come with or without alcohol. The beans must be certified as 'organic', of course, so look for the United States Department of Agriculture's 'USDA Organic' label in the United States; the label can be different in other parts of the world.

Imitation vanilla is made from synthetic materials such as wood pulp. Vanilla flavouring is normally a combination of synthetic and pure extract. The labels are unclear about the purity, so you should check the ingredients if you want to avoid purchasing the wrong type of vanilla flavouring. The best choice for a natural and clean flavour will be pure vanilla extract or organic premium vanilla extract, if you are avoiding alcohol. Well-known pure vanilla extract distributors in the U.S. and globally include Nielsen-Massey, McCormick, Simply Organic, The Vanilla Company, Penzeys Spices and The Watkins Company.

McCormick Pure Vanilla Extract, and Watkins double-strength 'Imitation vanilla essence'.

'A' grade vanilla beans are called gourmet beans. They are chocolatey-brown and measure 15 to 18 centimetres (6 to 7 in.) with 35 per cent moisture. 'B' grade beans are called extract beans and also measure 15 to 18 centimetres. They are dry to the touch with only 15 to 25 per cent moisture.

The best-quality vanilla beans are from Mexico. 'They have thin skin and a moisture level of 25% (those from Madagascar have 20%, and Java at 15% or less).'[7] High-quality Madagascar beans are as flavourful as the Mexican beans. Beans from Tahiti are not as flavourful due to the low levels of seeds in the pods. Beans from Bali are 'dry and brittle and very low in vanillin content'.[8] The grading for exports of cured beans falls into two categories, split and whole, and these are then sorted by grade.

A knife with scraped vanilla seeds.

Madagascar and Réunion beans should be rich in aroma with 2.9 per cent of vanillin. Indonesia ligneous should have a strong aroma and 2.7 per cent vanillin. Mexican beans should have a fine aroma with 1.8 per cent vanillin. The Tahitian variety should have a sweet, perfume-like aroma with 1.5 per cent vanillin. The quality of beans should be oily, chocolate brown in colour, well-formed.[9]

Packaging

A popular way to transport vanilla is by placing it in bundles inside tin cans lined with waxed paper, which are then placed into wooden boxes. The packaged cartons are stored in cool and ventilated areas. The beans are often sold in glass and plastic tubes.

Vanilla beans and synthetic vanilla are featured in numerous products. The following list, by Felix Buccellato, published in the *Handbook of Vanilla Science and Technology* (2011), is but a small selection of the major companies that use vanilla to enhance their manufactured foodstuffs and fragrances:

Food and Beverages

Pepsi	Smoothie King
Jim Beam	J&J Snack Foods Corporation
Coca-Cola	Dunkin' Brands
Unilever	Starbucks
Abbott	Hain Celestial Group
Nestlé	Jones Soda Company
Diageo	Boylan's Bottling Company
Spirits Marque One LLC	Cadbury
V&S Vin & Spirits AB	Schweppes

Women's Fragrances

Coty	Burberry
Guerlain	Jean Patou
Lauder	Sarah Jessica Parker
Yves Saint Laurent	Vera Wang
Calvin Klein	Britney Spears
Chanel	Houbigant

Men's Fragrances

Houbigant	Paco Rabanne
Dana Classic	New Dane
Fabergé	

Different Products

Vanilla bean paste contains specks of vanilla beans that have been ground into a paste. Vanilla powder is typically made from vanilla extract or flavouring, and will often contain starches as fillers.[10] Ground vanilla contains specks and pieces of ground beans, and only beans.

Storage

Once you decide to purchase high-quality beans, store them in an airtight container. If you are making extract, store them in alcohol. If looking to make vanilla sugar, store them in sugar. If the beans become dry, add a potato to the sugar. If they become too dry, soak them in water or milk for a few minutes. This process will soften the beans and make them easier to split open with a knife.

Flavour Enhancement

In the world of gastronomy, vanilla is primarily used as a flavour enhancement in baking and in sweets. Everything from medicine, bonbons and confectionery bars to ice cream and carbonated beverages features vanilla as a base flavour or flavour complement. Vanilla is also used to mask harsh or unpleasant tastes and aftertastes, particularly in cocoa and diet or low-fat products. Ever flexible and adaptable, it can also be employed in the unlikeliest of foods, including vegetables and poultry. Due to its various chemical compounds, you can easily utilize vanilla when cooking with tomatoes, corn, asparagus, dairy, chicken, potatoes or fennel.

COMMON COMPOUNDS	AROMAS	SHARE WITH OTHERS
Vanillin	Sweet, vanilla	Citrus, dill, fish, sherry
4-Hydroxybenzaldehyde Vanilla	Almond, balsamic, tomato	Beer, pineapple, shrimp
4-Anisaldehyde	Almond, anise, caramel, mint, popcorn, sweet	Basil, coffee, hazelnuts
2,3-Butanediol	Cream, floral, fruit, herb, onion	Cider, melon, pecans, vinegar
3-Hydroxy-2-Butanone	Butter, cream, green bell pepper	Barley, blue cheese, clams, honey
Acetovanillone	Clove, flower, vanilla	Beans, pork, soy sauce, wine

From James Briscione and Brooke Parkhurst, *The Flavor Matrix: The Art and Science of Pairing Common Ingredients to Create Extraordinary Dishes* (2018).[11]

Nielsen-Massey, a well-known importer of a number of flavours, created the following categories of vanilla's profile:

Mexican vanilla has a spicy and deep woody character that complements citrus fruits, cinnamon, cloves and spices. This vanilla is best used for ginger snaps and spice cookies. When cooking with it, it is best with barbecue sauces, chili and tomato sauce. Hot chocolate and chai lattes brings the best of this vanilla. Madagascar vanilla beans have a sweet and woody aroma. It's best used for cakes, cookies, ice cream, puddings and pastries. It also complements seafood, sauces, soups and marinades. This vanilla can give hot chocolate and teas a sweet and delicate earthy taste.

Tahitian vanilla aroma is floral, fruity, has an anise flavour. This vanilla is best adding it in pastry creams, fruit pies, sauces, smoothies, pudding and custards, salad dressings, sweet potato salad, fruit juices, martinis, margaritas, gin, vodka and rum.[12]

Flavour, which deeply affects our sense of taste, is, much like smell, tied to our emotions and feelings. Its importance in our lives cannot be overestimated. Yet, as with many other aspects of our existence, compromises often need to be considered. Should I purchase the BMW sedan or the Ford Compact? The Rolex or Timex? A premium vanilla extract, or the imitation variety? You can proudly wear Guerlain's Spiritueuse Double Vanille Eau de Parfum for your night on the town, or douse yourself with its cheaper knock-off purchased at the local pharmacy. Decisions are often dictated by budgetary concerns, and vanilla usage is no different. Chefs, bakers, perfumers, right down to the average person preparing a cake in their kitchen, deal with this reality on a daily basis. That being said, while there will always be a place for inexpensive alternatives, there simply is no substitute, taste-wise, for magnificent pure vanilla. It's worth it! There is little question that imitation vanilla options continue to make inroads in the marketplace. Yet, with consumers increasingly considering social, economic and health ramifications when making purchases, a future of pure vanilla continuing to enhance our lives seems assured.

Recipes

'Delicious perfume of vanilla'
– Jean Anthelme Brillat-Savarin, *Physiologie du Goût: Méditations de Gastronomie Transcendante* (1841)

Emotions, particularly those of nostalgia, can often be ignited by the smallest and most incidental things or items. These feelings can range from happiness to remorse and everything in between. From time to time, a person can become wary of the arrival of these sparked memories. Coming of age in the boroughs of New York City during the 1970s was wonderful and fascinating. I was just one of perhaps hundreds of thousands of newly arrived immigrants from the Caribbean islands who settled in various ethnic conclaves just a short distance from Manhattan. The apartments that my family and I resided in during this period were modest, with kitchens that were functional, if little else. These kitchens brought forth the magnificent smells and flavours that were deeply ingrained in my being and my culture. Many of my cherished memories revolve around the kitchen and the meals and desserts it produced. I hope that you will enjoy and be adventurous cooking the following recipes with my favourite flavour.

Surprisingly Delicious Food Pairings

Vanilla Scrambled Eggs

4 large eggs
1 tbsp milk
¼ tsp vanilla bean seeds
1 tbsp melted butter (you may substitute with neutral oil
or spray)
salt and pepper to taste

Break the eggs into a large bowl. Add the milk (you can substitute with non-dairy milk), vanilla seeds and salt and pepper to taste. Whisk the ingredients together. Lightly grease a pan with the butter or oil and heat, careful not to let it burn. Pour the mixture into the pan. Take a spatula and pull the outer edges to the centre of the pan, breaking up the cooked pieces and cook until they are mostly done. Turn off the heat, remove from pan, and serve.

Blanched Asparagus with Vanilla Lemon Vinaigrette

1 bundle of asparagus (around 400 g)
2 oz (60 ml) lemon juice
2 tbsp red wine vinegar
2 tbsp oil (rapeseed (canola) grapeseed or corn)
½ scraped vanilla pod
salt and pepper to taste

Prepare a large bowl of ice water. Using a large saucepan, add 8 cups (2 l) of water and bring to the boil. Cut off the 'woody' ends of the asparagus. Cook the asparagus in boiling water for about 2 to 3 minutes, depending on the thickness. Drain the asparagus in colander. Place them in the ice-water bowl until cooled.

In a small bowl, whisk the lemon juice, red wine vinegar, oil and vanilla pod. Drain the asparagus, dry and place on a platter. Spoon the vinaigrette over the asparagus. Add salt and pepper to taste.

Baked Sweet Potato Fries

2 lb (900 g) sweet potatoes, peeled
2 tbsp vegetable oil with neutral flavour
1 tsp vanilla seeds (scraped from a vanilla pod)
1 tsp salt
½ tsp black pepper

Preheat the oven to 350°F (175°C) and cut the sweet potatoes into sticks ½ in. (1½ cm) wide and 3 in. (8 cm) long. Toss them in a bowl with the oil. Combine the vanilla, salt and pepper into a small bowl, then add the mixture to the sweet potatoes. Spread the fries out on two rimmed baking sheets. Bake until brown and crisp on the bottom, about 15 to 20 minutes. Then, flip and cook until the other side is crisp, about 10 minutes. Serve warm.

Shellfish Vanilla Vinaigrette

½ tsp scraped vanilla pod
4 oz (120 ml) white or red wine vinegar
2 tbsp finely chopped shallots or white onion
1 tbsp coarsely ground white or black pepper

Place the vinegar and vanilla in a small bowl and whisk together. Add the shallots, black pepper and salt to taste. You can use this vinaigrette as a replacement for cocktail sauce with raw clams and oysters.

Sautéed Vegetables

1 tbsp olive oil
1 tbsp butter
1 clove garlic, finely chopped
½ shallot, chopped small
2 courgettes, cut in half lengthwise and sliced
1 yellow pepper cut into chunks
¼ tsp scraped vanilla pod
¼ tsp salt
ground pepper to taste

In a large heated skillet or frying pan, warm the oil and butter until the butter melts. Add the garlic and cook for 3 minutes. Add the shallot and cook for 4 minutes. Add the vegetables, vanilla, salt and pepper. Cook until tender, being careful not to overcook. Serve warm with your favourite meat dish.

Seared Chicken Breast, Poached Asparagus Tips, Tomato Basil Vanilla Cream Sauce
Recipe by Chef Jean F. Claude, Professor at
New York City College of Technology

4 skinless, boneless chicken breasts (4 oz / 112 g each)
2 oz (60 g) olive oil
2 oz (60 g) shallot, sliced
8 oz (240 ml) chicken stock
4 oz (120 ml) dry white wine
2 oz (60 g) tomato, skinned, seeded and diced
1 tbsp fresh basil
8 oz (240 ml) heavy (double) cream
1 vanilla pod
4 oz (110 g) butter
8 oz (230 g) fresh asparagus
salt and pepper to taste

Preheat the oil in a large skillet or frying pan over a medium-high heat. Season the chicken with salt and white pepper. When the oil is hot, add the chicken breast thickest side down first. Cook for 2 minutes until the chicken is golden brown. Turn the chicken over to the other side and continue to cook for another 3 to 4 minutes until the chicken is almost cooked. Remove from the pan and finish in the oven at 350°F (180°C). Cook for about 22 minutes. Place a thermometer inside the meat and make sure the internal temperature is 165°F (75°C) before serving.

Tomato basil vanilla cream sauce (1 oz/28 g of sauce per portion)
In a heavy bottom saucepan, add the shallots and wine and reduce. Trim the asparagus, keeping just the tips. Add the chicken to the saucepan and simmer. Poach the asparagus for 2 minutes in the chicken stock. Remove the asparagus and set aside. Add the heavy/double cream to the saucepan and continue to simmer until reduced. Split the vanilla pod in half lengthwise, scrape the seeds with the back of a knife, and add the seeds to the simmering cream. Remove the sauce from the heat and whisk in the butter slowly to form the sauce. Roll the basil leaves into a cigar shape and cut it into thin strips. Add the diced tomato and basil to the sauce. Finish with salt and pepper. Take out the chicken breast, slice and place it over the asparagus with the tips facing the top of the plate. Ladle 1 oz (30 g) of sauce over the chicken for each person.
Serves 4

Chopped Tomatoes in Syrup

½ lb (225 g) tomatoes (not too ripe)
16 oz (450 ml) water
16 oz (450 g) sugar
1 tsp pure vanilla extract
1 small cinnamon stick
pinch of salt
raisins (optional)

Slice an 'X' into the bottom of each tomato using a paring knife. Lower tomatoes into a pot of boiling water and blanch for 15 to 30 seconds. Use a slotted spoon to remove the tomatoes from the pot. Plunge into an ice-water bath until cool enough to handle, about 30 seconds. Peel each tomato (you will see cracks on the skin). Slice the tomatoes in half and remove the seeds, then chop the tomatoes and place them in a bowl. Combine the water and sugar and cook in a saucepan until the sugar is dissolved. The syrup should feel heavy when you pull up the spoon. Add the vanilla, salt, cinnamon stick and raisins, if desired. Add the chopped tomatoes to the mixture and cook for about 5 minutes. Let it cool to room temperature, then serve.

Vanilla and Chocolate Chip Pancakes

16 oz (450 g) all-purpose (plain) flour
2 tsp baking powder
1 ½ tsp baking soda (bicarbonate of soda)
2 tsp sugar
½ tsp salt
2 large eggs, slightly beaten
14 oz (420 ml) whole milk (or substitute of your preference)
2 tsp unsalted butter, melted and cooled
2 tbsp pure vanilla extract
2 oz (60 ml) melted butter (or neutral vegetable oil)
2 oz (112 g) chocolate chips
warmed syrup

In a large bowl, sift together the flour, baking powder, baking soda and salt. Stir in the sugar, and make a well in the centre. Pour the eggs, milk, vanilla and melted butter into the well. Gradually whisk from the centre outward until the ingredients are well combined but still a little lumpy. Do not over-mix the batter, or the pancakes will be heavy. Very gently stir in the chocolate chips. Preheat a non-stick pan over a medium-high heat. Brush the pan with melted butter or oil. Slowly ladle ¼ cup (110 g) of batter onto the centre of the pan, so it spreads out into a circle on its own. After about 2 minutes, the pancake will begin to bubble in the centre, and a few bubbles will have popped. This means that the underside is golden and ready to flip. Use a spatula to flip the pancake. Cook until the second side is golden, about 1 minute longer, then transfer to a heatproof plate. Repeat with each pancake. Serve with warm syrup.

Broiled Salmon with Honey, Balsamic Vinegar and Vanilla Glaze

Recipe adapted from Janet Sawyer, *Vanilla: Cooking with One of the World's Finest Ingredients: Cooking with the King of Spices*

3 oz (80 g) salmon fillets
2 tsp olive oil
1 tsp clear honey
1 tsp vanilla seeds/paste
salt
ground pepper to taste
4 oz (115 g) mixed baby greens
2 tbsp olive oil
1 tbsp red wine vinegar

Make a glaze by combining the olive oil, clear honey, vanilla seeds and salt in a small bowl. Place the salmon in a shallow dish. Brush the glaze on the salmon and let it marinate for 1 or 2 hours. Place the salmon under a hot grill/broiler for about 10 minutes until the glaze forms a crust on the skin and the salmon is cooked all the way through, yet is still moist. In a separate small bowl, whisk together two tablespoons of olive oil and red wine vinegar. Add salt and pepper to taste. Place the mixed baby greens in a medium bowl, drizzle the vinaigrette over the greens and toss. Place the salmon fillets on individual plates and serve with baby greens on the side.

Fresh Strawberry and Spinach Salad

Recipe adapted from Georgeanne Brennan, *Williams-Sonoma Salad of the Day: 365 Recipes for Every Day of the Year*

16 oz (450 g) baby spinach
4 oz (110 g) strawberries (halved)

For the vinaigrette
2 tbsp rapeseed/canola oil (or any neutral oil of your preference)
2 tbsp balsamic vinegar
½ tsp vanilla seeds or ¼ tsp pure vanilla extract
salt and pepper to taste

In a small bowl, combine the oil, vinegar, vanilla, salt and pepper until well blended. Place the spinach and strawberries in a medium bowl. Drizzle the vinaigrette over the spinach and strawberries until they are well coated. Add salt and/or pepper to taste.

Dominican Quesillo (Flan)

My mother's recipe

For the caramel
8 oz (224 g) sugar
4 oz (120 ml) water

Mix the sugar and water and cook in a heavy saucepan over high heat for five minutes until it simmers and then low heat until thick, golden caramel syrup forms. Make sure it does not burn! Pour the caramel carefully into a 10 in. (25 cm) shallow pan and spread over the bottom of the pan by moving it around until the bottom and the sides of the pan are coated.

For the flan
5 egg yolks
8 oz (240 ml) evaporated milk

8 oz (224 g) sweetened condensed milk
1 tsp vanilla extract
2 tbsp raisins
pinch of salt

Topping (optional)
1 tbsp water
½ tsp vanilla extract
2 oz (112 g) pineapple preserves

Preheat the oven to 163°C (325°F). Mix together the egg yolks, sweetened condensed milk and evaporated milk. Stir in the vanilla and sieve the mixture to get rid of undissolved egg parts. Add the raisins. Pour the mixture carefully into the shallow baking pan, trying not to disturb the caramel layer. Bake in a hot water bath. (Take a larger, deep baking pan and fill it halfway with water, then place the pan with the flan mixture inside. Be sure the water does not spill over.) Bake for 2 hours 20 minutes. To check for doneness, insert a toothpick to its centre until it comes out clean. Cool down to room temperature. To loosen edges of the flan, use a dinner knife. Then, place a serving plate on top of the pan (one which will retain the syrup) and flip it over. (You will hear the flan drop onto the dish.) Mix the pineapple preserves and vanilla extract with a tablespoon of water. Spread it over the top of the flan. Place the finished flan in the refrigerator for about an hour. Serve chilled.

Rice Pudding
This is my own family recipe

⅓ cup (75 g) long grain white rice
24 oz (700 ml) milk or evaporated milk (or a non-dairy milk
of your choice)
¼ cup (56 g) sugar
pinch of salt
1 tbsp pure vanilla extract

1 cinnamon stick (or ½ tsp ground vanilla)
1 in. (2½ cm) lime or lemon peel with no white membrane
(optional)
2 oz (56 g) raisins (optional)

Wash the rice. In a medium saucepan, combine the rice, milk, lime
or lemon peel, salt and cinnamon. Cook the rice over a medium
heat for about 20 to 25 minutes until the rice is tender. (Stir to pre-
vent the rice from sticking to the saucepan.) Once cooked, remove
the lime/lemon peel and cinnamon stick. Mix in the sugar, vanilla
extract and raisins, and cook for another 5 minutes. Let the rice
pudding cool down. Serve in small bowls.

Quick Vanilla Pudding

8 oz (240 ml) whole milk
1 egg yolk
1½ tsp sugar
1 tsp pure vanilla extract
1 tbsp cornflour (cornstarch)
pinch of salt

Place all of the ingredients in a small saucepan and whisk together
until blended. Place the saucepan on a medium heat and stir the
mixture until it starts to thicken. Once the mixture is cooked,
remove from the heat. Spoon the pudding into small bowls and
place it in the refrigerator to cool and serve in ten minutes. Once
cooled, serve as a dessert or snack.

Orange Vanilla Vinaigrette

juice from two oranges
1 tbsp apple cider vinegar
8 oz (240 ml) olive oil
4 drops hot sauce

1 tsp honey
1 ½ tsp vanilla extract
juice from 1 lemon
¼ tsp salt
black pepper to taste

Place the orange juice, vinegar, olive oil, hot sauce, vanilla, honey, lemon juice, salt and pepper in a bowl. Whisk the vinaigrette until well blended. This vinaigrette can be served with mixed greens (romaine lettuce, oak leaf lettuce, frisée and radicchio).

Vanilla Cupcakes (with Powdered Sugar or Frosting)

Recipe by Pastry Chef Thalia Pericles, Assistant Professor at New York City College of Technology

16 oz (448 g) all-purpose (plain) flour
10 oz (336 g) granulated sugar
1 tsp (4 g) salt
1 tsp baking soda (bicarbonate of soda)
2 whole eggs
2 tbsp pure vanilla extract
8 oz (240 ml) buttermilk
1 ½ tsp pure vanilla extract
1 ⅔ cup (400 ml) vegetable oil
1 tsp white vinegar
⅓ cup (75 g) powdered (icing) sugar (for dusting the cupcakes)

Preheat oven to 175°C (350°F). Line two muffin pans with paper liners. Combine and sift the flour, sugar, baking soda and salt into a large mixing bowl. In another large mixing bowl, whisk together the eggs, vanilla, buttermilk, vegetable oil and vinegar. Make a well in the middle of the dry ingredients and add the wet ingredients to the well. Mix all ingredients together until combined. (Some lumps are fine; mixing it until smooth is over-mixing.) Carefully divide the batter equally among the 24 muffin cups. Each liner should be about half full. Bake for about 22 to 25 minutes, until you insert a toothpick in the centre and it comes out clean, or when the cupcake springs back to the touch. Remove from the oven and let the pan cool for 5 minutes. Remove the cupcakes, place them on a wire rack and allow to cool completely. Place the (icing) sugar in a sifter and dust over the cupcakes, or decorate with frosting.

Frosting
16 oz (450 g) powdered (icing) sugar, sifted
1½ tbsp milk
1 tsp pure vanilla extract
⅛ tsp salt
14 tbsp (200 g) unsalted butter, cut into cubes

Using a stand mixer fitted with a paddle attachment, place the sugar in a bowl. Add the milk, salt and mix on a low speed until the sugar is evenly blended. To moisten the mixture (it will look dry), add the butter and gradually increase the speed from low to medium to high. Beat until fluffy and light in texture, about 3 to 4 minutes. Add in the vanilla extract during the last minute. Frost the cupcakes when cooled.
Makes 24 cupcakes

Thomas Jefferson Ice Cream
Adapted from Jefferson Papers, Library of Congress
www.monticello.org/thomas-jefferson

64 fl. oz (2 l) heavy (double) cream
1 cup (225 g) sugar
1 vanilla pod
6 egg yolks

In a large, heavy saucepan, combine the cream and sugar. Split the vanilla bean in half lengthwise. With a sharp knife, scrape the seeds into a pan, then add the bean. In a saucepan, place the cream mixture on a medium heat until bubbles form around the sides of the pan. Stir in the sugar to dissolve. In a small bowl, whisk the egg yolks until pale yellow. Add small amounts of the hot mixture slowly to the egg mixture and keep whisking until all of it is incorporated. Place the mixture back into saucepan. Cook over a low heat until the mixture is just thick enough to coat a metal spoon and the temperature reaches 160°F (70°C), stirring constantly. Do not allow it to boil. Immediately transfer to a bowl. Place the bowl in a pan of ice water. Stir gently and occasionally for 2 minutes. Discard the vanilla bean. Press waxed paper onto the surface of the custard. Refrigerate for several hours or overnight. Take the bowl out of the refrigerator. Then, use an ice cream freezer cylinder and fill it up so it's two-thirds full. Follow the ice cream manufacturer's directions for freezing the custard. Transfer the ice cream to a freezer container, and freeze for 4 to 6 hours or until firm. Repeat the steps with any leftover mixture in the ice cream maker.

Vanilla Sugar

16 oz (450 g) granulated sugar
1 or 2 vanilla beans (can be a bean already split from
a previous recipe)

Place the sugar and bean(s) in a tightly lidded container. Store in a cool, dark place for two days.

Grandma's Cream Cheese Pie
Recipe by pastry chef Susan Lifrieri-Lowry, Assistant Professor at
New York City College of Technology

For the crust
7 double graham crackers or digestive biscuits, crushed (if you
do not have graham crackers, then you'll need to add ½ tsp
ground cinnamon to the digestive biscuits)
3 tbsp melted butter
1 tbsp sugar

Mix the graham cracker (digestive biscuit) crumbs, sugar and melted butter until wet. Press the mixture into an 8-in. (20 cm) pie plate, reserving ¼ cup (110 g) of crumbs for later use. Bake at 350°F (180°C) for 8 to 10 minutes until fragrant.

For the filling
¾ lb (340 g) cream cheese
2 eggs
4 oz (110 g) sugar
1 tsp vanilla extract
1 vanilla bean (seeds only – reserve pod for another use)

Mix together the cream cheese and sugar until smooth. Add the eggs, one at a time, then vanilla seeds and extract. Pour on top of the crust. Bake at 375°F (190°C) for about 15 to 20 minutes until almost set.

For the sour cream topping
8 fl. oz (30 ml) sour cream
2 tbsp sugar
½ tsp of vanilla extract, plus the seeds from ½ a vanilla pod

Mix together the sugar, sour cream and vanilla bean and extract. Pour the mixture on top of the cream cheese mixture and sprinkle the reserved crumbs on top. Bake at 350°F (175°C) for another 8 minutes. Cool completely before slicing.

Orange and Cream Cooler

8 oz (240 ml) orange juice
2 oz (50 g) sugar
16 oz (480 ml) evaporated milk (or half-and-half or a substitute of your choice)
8 oz (225 g) crushed ice, divided into two parts
½ tsp pure vanilla extract

In a pitcher, combine the orange juice and sugar and mix until the sugar dissolves. Add the milk and vanilla. Add ½ cup (110 g) of ice and stir until cold. Place ½ cup (110 g) of ice in a tall glass. Pour the cooler into the glass and serve immediately.

Cream of Corn Soup
Adapted from Mely Martínez

20 oz (560 g) frozen or fresh sweetcorn kernels (removed from the cob)
2 tbsp butter
⅓ cup (75 g) white onion, finely chopped
2 cloves garlic, diced
16 oz (480 ml) chicken broth or stock
½ in. (6 cm) split vanilla pod
2 cups (480 ml) whole milk
1 tbsp all-purpose (plain) flour
4 oz (110 g) Mexican queso fresco cheese (or mozzarella), cut into cubes
4 tbsp heavy (double) cream for garnish (optional)
salt and pepper to taste

Pull off the cornhusks from the fresh sweetcorn and remove. Cut the kernels using a sharp knife; be careful to remove only the grains. Melt the butter in a saucepan over medium-low heat. Add the onion and garlic. Cook, stirring to avoid sticking to the bottom until the onion and garlic are softened but not browned, about 5 minutes. Increase the heat to medium-high. Add the corn, chicken broth and vanilla bean and bring to a simmer. Reduce the heat to medium-low and gently simmer for 15 minutes, or until the corn is tender. Once the corn is cooked, remove about 4 oz (110 g) of the kernels with a slotted spoon and reserve for garnishing. While the soup simmers, mix the flour and milk in a separate bowl. Mix well to avoid lumps. Place the milk-and-flour mixture into a blender. Remove the vanilla bean from the corn and add the cooked corn kernels with the broth. Process the soup until smooth. Return the puréed soup to the saucepan and simmer over a medium heat until it's hot and the soup thickens, about 5 more minutes. Stir the soup to avoid sticking to the pan. It should have a thick consistency. Season with salt and pepper to taste. Serve soup in bowls and garnish with reserved corn kernels and cubes of cheese.

Milkshake and Fries

For the fries
3 large baking potatoes (3 lb/1.5 kg)
3 tbsp vegetable oil
1 tsp salted water
salt and pepper to taste

Preheat the oven to 350°F (175°C). Wash and cut the potatoes, then slice into ¼-in. (6.35 mm) wide wedges. (Peeling the potatoes is optional.) Place the sliced potatoes in a bowl of cold salted water and leave for about 10 minutes. Drain the potatoes and dry them with paper towels. In a bowl toss them with the oil. Cover an ovenproof dish with aluminium foil, or use a non-stick sheet and spread fries evenly over it. Bake for 25 minutes or until golden brown. Once cooked, take them out and place them in a bowl. Toss them with a sprinkle of salt and pepper.

For the milkshake
8 oz (225 g) vanilla ice cream
12 oz (180 ml) whole milk
½ tsp vanilla extract
1 tbsp honey (optional)

Add the milk, vanilla extract, honey and ice cream in a blender. Blend until smooth and creamy, then pour in a glass.

And yes, you can and *should* dip the fries in the milkshake – it tastes delicious!

Beverages

Vanilla-infused Tea

From Laura Fronty, *Aromatic Teas and Herbal Infusions*

1 teabag of black tea
1 vanilla bean, diced
8 fl. oz (240 ml) water

Bring water to a boil and pour over the black tea. Add the vanilla and let it steep for 4 minutes.

Vanilla Simple Syrup

8 oz (225 g) granulated sugar
8 fl. oz (240 ml) water
1 vanilla bean, split lengthwise

Combine the water and sugar in a small saucepan over a medium heat, stirring gently. Bring to a boil for about 1 minute, long enough for the sugar to dissolve completely. Add the vanilla bean and let the mixture cool for about 15 minutes. Once cooled, place the mixture in a sealed glass container and store in the refrigerator.

Mojito

2 oz (60 ml) white rum (whichever brand suits your preference)
½ oz (15 ml) vanilla simple syrup, see recipe above
¾ oz (20 ml) lime juice
3 sprigs of fresh mint
1 lime wedge
4 drops of club soda (soda water)
4 oz (120 g) ice

Combine the rum, vanilla simple syrup, lime juice, mint and ice in a cocktail shaker. Shake until well combined. Pour into a glass. Top off with club soda and serve with a lime wedge.

Bourbon Martini

2 oz (60 ml) bourbon (whichever brand suits your preference)
1 oz (30 ml) vanilla simple syrup, see recipe above
¾ oz (20 ml) triple sec
1 orange peel (optional)
1 vanilla bean (optional)
4 oz (120 g) ice

Place the ingredients in a cocktail shaker with ½ cup of ice and stir until blended. Strain and pour into a chilled martini glass. Garnish with a vanilla bean or orange twist.

Summer Punch

1 oz (30 ml) vanilla simple syrup, see recipe above
4 oz (120 g) mixed berries (frozen)
8 oz (240 ml) water
8 oz (240 ml) ginger soda
4 oz (120 g) ice

Combine all the ingredients in a glass pitcher. Serve chilled.

Vanilla-infused Vodka

24 oz (750 ml) vodka (whichever brand suits your preference)
1 vanilla bean
1 lemon peel (optional)

Pour the vodka into a lidded glass bottle (the original vodka bottle works fine). Add the vanilla bean and the peel from one lemon (optional). Close and let it infuse for 1 to 2 weeks in a cool, dark place, gently shaking every other day.

Mexican Chocolate
Barbara Hansen, *Mexican Cookery*

24 oz (720 ml) milk
3 oz (85 g) semi-sweet chocolate (for best results, buy Mexican chocolate)
2 tbsp sugar
½ tsp ground cinnamon
¼ tsp vanilla extract
1 oz (30 ml) tequila or Grand Marnier (optional)
whipped cream (optional)

Place the milk, chocolate, vanilla, cinnamon and sugar into a medium saucepan over medium heat. Bring the contents to a boil, but don't allow the milk to overflow. When the chocolate is soft, beat the mixture with a wire whisk or fork. Allow the mixture to boil again until it starts foaming. Remove saucepan from heat. Serve, pouring immediately into mugs. Add some tequila or Grand Marnier and place a dollop of whipped cream into each cup.

Products You Can Make at Home

Vanilla Oil

To be used for cooking or as a perfume.

4 oz (120 ml) almond oil (any oil with no scent)
1 split vanilla bean

Place all the oil and split vanilla bean into a medium-sized Mason jar, seal and shake. Place the jar on a windowsill where the sun will heat up the jar. Leave it for about 4 weeks. Using a colander, strain the oil through a coffee filter and place the oil into a small jar. Store in a cool place; this oil will last for a month.

Facial Scrub

4 oz (110 g) brown sugar
2 oz (60 ml) sweet almond oil
2 oz (60 ml) vanilla oil, see recipe above

Mix all the ingredients together with a spoon. Apply, gently rubbing mixture all around your face. Wash your face with warm water until all the scrub is gone and towel dry.

Facial Mask

3 tbsp yoghurt
½ tsp vanilla oil, see recipe above

Mix all the yoghurt and vanilla oil together in a small bowl. Apply the mixture to the face and leave mixture on for 15 minutes. Wash with warm water until the mask is gone and towel dry.

Air Freshener

24 fl. oz (720 ml) cold water
1 tbsp vanilla extract
1 cinnamon stick

Place the water in a small saucepan on a medium heat until it comes to a boil. Lower heat and let the water simmer with vanilla and cinnamon for about half an hour. Discard once the mixture cools.

Global Vanilla

Africa

Vanilla is currently grown in several African nations, including Tanzania, Kenya and the Eastern Democratic Republic of the Congo, but it is Uganda that lays claim to having the most successful and productive industry on the continent. Introduced in 1918 while Uganda was under British control, farmers of all nationalities and races leased farmland to grow coffee, rubber and cotton. They would then incorporate vanilla into their plantations by attaching vanilla vines to other plants and bushes. Uganda also benefits from its association with the American McCormick Company that began in the 1960s and continues today. Assisted by McCormick's knowledge and guidance, Uganda now produces some of the finest vanilla in the world. The orchid is now grown in more than a dozen regions, principally located near Lake Victoria and along the Nile River.

Australia and Papua New Guinea

Australia's modest yet award-winning vanilla industry is primarily located in Queensland in the Northern Territories. This region offers a fine microclimate similar to that of its northern neighbour Papua New Guinea, which also produces vanilla but without the amenities that Australia's industry enjoys. That said, Papua New Guinea's annual crop output dwarfs Australia's, and it is

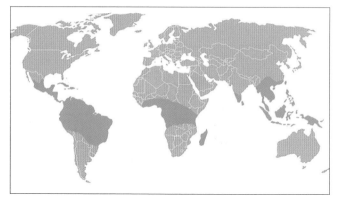

Vanilla's worldwide production, shown by green-shaded regions.

currently the fifth largest producer in the world. Vanilla produced in Australia is typically of the *V. planifolia* variety, and augmented by limited amounts of *V. tahitensis*.

Central and South America

In Costa Rica, wild vanilla has grown in abundance for hundreds of years. Central America has the ideal growing environment for the vine to thrive. Central and South American farmers had taken advantage of the hand pollination system to farm the beans. The farmers face the same problems as in any other country that produces vanilla: keeping track of how many fruits each vine will produce and making sure the soil is rich and healthy. Despite the discovery of a similar vanilla species, *V. planifolia* is the preferred choice. Guatemala and Belize have grown wild vanilla since the days of the Mayan Empire. Today, vanilla is a more prominent crop for export in Central America. In Peru, wild vanilla grows in the Amazon, and only small amounts of it are exported.

China

China entered the vanilla market in 1991 and is now the third highest producer in the world, although its emergence has thus far failed to have much impact when it comes to supply and, consequently, price. China's vanilla industry was initially hindered by Madagascar's decision to deregulate prices, causing prices to dip significantly. Things have improved recently, as China, which had previously grown vanilla only for domestic purposes, has begun exporting it as well. Its major areas of vanilla production are Xishuangbanna, located in the southwestern Yunnan Province near the Vietnamese border, and Hainan Island. The Chinese use two distinct techniques for vanilla pollination: the traditional method devised and implemented on Réunion Island, and the modern system known as the 'removing method', which strips away the cap-like rostellum directly and presses the pollen mass so that it adheres to the stigma.

French Polynesia

The Society Islands are an archipelago located within the South Pacific Ocean. Modest vanilla production occurs on several small islands, including Taha'a, known as 'Vanilla Island', Moorea, Marquesas and, most notably, Tahiti. Although newer generations of growers on these islands have begun to adopt modern cultivation and processing methods, production levels remain fairly low.

Guadeloupe and Martinique

Members of the Lesser Antilles group of islands in the Caribbean Sea, Guadeloupe and Martinique are home to several impressive plantations which primarily produce *V. pompona* for the fragrance industry.

Vanilla grown on vines in an artificial greenhouse environment.

India

V. planifolia was introduced into this country in 1835 by the British, who planted it in small farms for their own use. Attempts to grow the industry in India stalled until the 1940s, when research overseen by the Kallar Fruit Research Station, located in the Nilgiris district, began producing results. During the 1990s, India's government-subsidized Spices Board encouraged vanilla cultivation, finding a wide variety of farmers eager to take up vanilla. By the turn of the century, overproduction had become an issue, and production rates have slowed somewhat. India's rapidly growing tourism and export businesses should have positive effects for its vanilla industry.

Indonesia

Indonesia is the largest island chain in the world, and encompasses more than 18,000 individual isles and atolls. Its history is marked by turmoil, upheaval, foreign intervention and political unrest, yet it is currently still the world's second largest producer of vanilla. The vine is assumed to have been introduced in 1817 by the Dutch, who proceeded to plant it in Bogor Botanical Gardens, one of the oldest gardens in Southeast Asia. Indonesia's main areas of vanilla cultivation are Bali, which began growing it in the early 1970s and at one point in the 1980s matched Madagascar in production, and South Java. Production of vanilla in Indonesia has fallen recently, as the government has encouraged and propped up its burgeoning tourism industry to the detriment of vanilla production.

Madagascar

Madagascar, the fourth largest island in the world, is located 400 kilometres (250 mi.) east of southern Africa. The island contains a remarkable array of trees, flowers and vegetation unlike those of any other region on the planet. The lush, tropical climate is ideal for vanilla production. The Sava region, located in the northeastern part of the island, consists of numerous small cities, including Antalaha, Vohemar, Andapa and Sambava, the towns for which Sava is an acronym. Sava is considered to be the capital of vanilla production, and vanilla is its main export crop. Interestingly, the indigenous Malagasy have never developed a taste for vanilla, and it has never been assimilated into their food, medicines or their culture in general. Vanilla products are almost exclusively enjoyed in tourist locations.

Farmers and producers have a low standard of living and typically work long hours taking care of their precious vines. Vanilla farmers and their families normally reside in very small villages of a few hundred people, and they have to deal with poorly maintained roads and a lack of running water, sanitation and electricity. Hospitals and schools are also scarce outside of major cities. Men, women and children of all ages spend the majority of their day pollinating thousands of flowers with modified bamboo sticks.

Even with vanilla prices approaching those of precious metals like silver and gold, farmers rarely benefit as much as the middlemen who purchase the green beans inexpensively from them, although they've become savvier over the last decade. The current high price of vanilla beans has brought a considerable amount of crime and corruption to the island in the form of theft and money laundering. Desperate farmers have lost their lives protecting the vines from thieves, while perpetrators are sometimes killed in the process of stripping the vines bare. Larger wholesalers have been forced to implement drastic security measures to stem theft, such as subjecting workers to full body checks before they exit the warehouses. As of 2019, prices of vanilla have stabilized somewhat, although they remain historically high. Unpredictable and drastic weather events will continue to be the primary cause of boom and bust in Madagascar's vanilla industry.

Mexico

Currently, vanilla production still thrives in the state of Veracruz, Mexico. However, due to the arduous process and long growing season, some farmers turn to growing other crops that are easy to cultivate and sold much quicker. Deforestation has eliminated the trees where vanilla once thrived, and climate change has brought hotter temperatures, causing the farmers to plant the vines at higher altitudes. Nonetheless, Mexico is still one of the top exporters of vanilla beans.

Réunion Island

Formerly known as Bourbon Island, this was the very first island in the Indian Ocean to grow vanilla. Réunion is located approximately 800 kilometres (500 mi.) to the east of Madagascar. French-run agricultural facilities operate there to this day. Vanilla production is typically managed by both cooperatives and privately owned plantations. Harsh weather conditions, along with blight and high labour costs, have severely curtailed vanilla production over the last hundred years as production has moved to its island neighbour Madagascar. When visiting this island, sample their local dish 'duck in vanilla'.

United States

Hawaii

Humble attempts to kick-start vanilla production on the Hawaiian islands have met with modest success at best, but an increasingly large number of entrepreneurs feel that, with a little nurturing, the potential to accommodate niche markets, such as the organics market, is clearly there. However, high production costs relative to other vanilla-growing regions could hinder their plans.

Florida

According to Dr Alan Chambers, Assistant Professor at the University of Florida/Institute of Food and Agricultural Sciences Tropical Research and Educational Center in Homestead,

> researchers are conducting studies at the moment to see if the Southern part of this state has a viable future for vanilla production. The weather is a key factor, and native orchid vines give a good indication of this state becoming a future vanilla producer.[1]

Puerto Rico

In 1909 the United States federal government began experimenting with vanilla production in the region of Mayagüez, located on the western part of the island of Puerto Rico. These tests ended in failure, however, due to a succession of hurricanes that ravaged Puerto Rico during the 1950s. Vanilla production never completely vanished, though, and because of the current high prices, production is predicted to increase over the next decade.

Samoa

Vanilla production remains quite limited in the country of Samoa, consisting of several islands in the Pacific Ocean. Presently, only a few farmers still participate in the growing of vanilla, down from over sixty growers only a decade ago. Labour intensity and the length of time it takes to bring vanilla beans to market were contributing factors in this sharp decline. Samoa's government has been attempting to persuade locals that 'a bucket of vanilla beans' is worth more than 'a truck full of coconuts'. Revitalization efforts have met with middling success.

References

1 Biology

1 Ken Cameron, *Vanilla Orchids: Natural History and Cultivation* (Portland, OR, 2011), p. 14.
2 Ibid., pp. 7–8.
3 Séverine Bory et al., 'Biodiversity and Preservation of Vanilla: Present State of Knowledge', *Genetic Resources and Crop Evolution*, LV/4 (June 2008), pp. 551–71.
4 Patricia Rain, *Vanilla: The Cultural History of the World's Most Popular Flavor and Fragrance* (New York, 2004), p. 79.
5 Ibid., p. 119.
6 J. Hernández-Hernández, 'Mexican Vanilla Production', in *Handbook of Vanilla Science and Technology*, 2nd edn, ed. D. Havkin-Frenkel and F. C. Belanger (Hoboken, NJ, 2011), p. 6.
7 Tim Ecott, *Vanilla: Travels in Search of the Ice Cream Orchid* (New York, 2004), p. xiii.
8 Patricia Rain, *Vanilla Cookbook* (Berkeley, CA, 1986), p. 12.
9 Patrick G. Hoffman and Charles M. Zapf, 'Flavor, Quality, and Authentication', in *Handbook of Vanilla Science and Technology*, ed. Havkin-Frenkel and Belanger, p. 163.

2 History and Origins

1 Santiago R. Ramirez et al., 'Dating the Origin of the Orchidaceae from a Fossil Orchid with Its Pollinator', *Nature*, CDXL/7157 (30 August 2007), p. 1042.

2 Patricia Rain, *Vanilla: The Cultural History of the World's Most Popular Flavor and Fragrance* (New York, 2004), p. 14.

3 Douglas T. Peck, 'The Geographical Origin and Acculturation of Maya Advanced Civilization in Mesoamerica', *Revista de Historia de América*, CXXX (2002), p. 26.

4 Lynn V. Foster, *Handbook to Life in the Ancient Maya World* (New York, 2002), p. 127.

5 Erasmo Curti-Diaz, *Cultivo y beneficiado de la vainilla en Mexico. Folleto technico para productores* (Papantla, Veracruz, 1995), p. 96.

6 Rain, *Vanilla*, p. 92.

7 Stuart B. Schwartz, *Victors and Vanquished: Spanish and Nahua Views of the Conquest of Mexico* (New York, 2000), pp. 5–6.

8 Francisco López de Gómara, *Historia general de las Indias y Vida de Hernán Cortés* (Caracas, 1979).

9 Camilla Townsend, 'Burying the White Gods: New Perspectives on the Conquest of Mexico', *American Historical Review*, CVIII/3 (June 2003), pp. 659–97.

10 Rain, *Vanilla*, p. 47.

11 Emilio Kouri, *A Pueblo Divided: Property, and Community in Papantla, Mexico* (Stanford, CA, 2004), p. 21.

12 Cited ibid., p. 47.

13 Mei Chin, 'Casanova: A Man's Healthy Appetite with All Life's Pleasures', www.irishtimes.com, 13 February 2018.

14 Elizabeth de Feydeau, *Jean-Louis Fargeon, Parfumeur de Marie-Antoinette* (Versailles, 2005).

15 Rain, *Vanilla*, p. 64.

3 Exporting the Vines

1 Sarah Lohman, 'The Marriage of Vanilla',
   www.laphamsquarterly.org, 4 January 2017.
2 Hannah Glasse, *The Art of Cookery* [1747], www.archive.org,
   accessed 24 December 2015, p. 342.
3 Mary Randolph, *The Virginia Housewife* (Baltimore, MD,
   1824), p. 143.
4 'Coca Cola', https://en.wikipedia.org, accessed
   4 March 2019.
5 Mary Bellis, 'The History of the Soda Fountain',
   www.thoughtco.com, 12 February 2019.
6 James Harvey Young, 'Three Atlanta Pharmacists', *Pharmacy
   in History*, XXXI/1 (1989), pp. 16–17.

4 The Modern World

1 Matt Siegel, 'How Ice Cream Helped America at War',
   www.theatlantic.com, 6 August 2017.
2 Dina Spector, 'The Twinkie Changed for Good Thanks
   to World War II', www.businessinsider.com, 17 November
   2012.
3 Patricia Rain, *Vanilla: The Cultural History of the World's Most
   Popular Flavor and Fragrance* (New York, 2004), p. 273.
4 Ibid.

5 Supply and Production

1 'Vanilla', https://oec.world/en/profile/hs92/0905,
   2 June 2019.
2 James Burton, 'The Leading Countries in Vanilla Production
   in the World', www.worldatlas.com, 9 August 2018.

6 Pop Culture

1 Joseph Lanza, *Vanilla Pop: Sweet Sounds from Frankie Avalon to ABBA* (Chicago, IL, 2005).

2 Mickey Hess, 'Hip-hop Realness and the White Performer', *Critical Studies in Media Communication*, XXII/5 (December 2005), p. 373.

7 Flavour Profile

1 A. S. Ranadive, 'Quality Control of Vanilla Beans and Extracts', in *Handbook of Vanilla Science and Technology*, ed. D. Havkin-Frenkel and F. C. Belanger (Hoboken, NJ, 2011), p. 145.

2 Ibid.

3 Patricia Rain, *Vanilla Cookbook* (Berkeley, CA, 1986), p. 7.

4 Ibid., p. 7.

5 Ibid.

6 C. Rose Kennedy and Kaitlyn Choi, 'The Flavor Rundown: Natural vs Artificial Flavors', http://sitn.hms.harvard.edu, 21 September 2015.

7 Javier De La Cruz Medina, Guadalupe C. Rodriguez Jiménez and Hugo S. García, 'Vanilla: Post-harvest Operations', www.fao.org, 16 June 2009.

8 Janet Sawyer, *Vanilla: Cooking with One of the World's Finest Ingredients* (London, 2014).

9 Medina et al., 'Vanilla: Post-harvest Operations'.

10 F. Buccellato, 'Vanilla in Perfumery and Beverages', in *Handbook of Vanilla Science and Technology*, ed. Havkin-Frenkel and Belanger, pp. 237–9.

11 James Briscione and Brooke Parkhurst, *The Flavor Matrix: The Art and Science of Pairing Common Ingredients to Create Extraordinary Dishes* (New York, 2018), p. 246.

12 See https://nielsenmassey.com/vanillas-and-flavors, 17 January 2019.

Global Vanilla

1   Alan Chambers, 'Potential for Commercial Vanilla
    Production in Southern Florida', https://crec.ifas.ufl.edu,
    accessed 1 June 2019.

Bibliography

'A Not-so-plain History of Vanilla', www.braums.com,
    19 June 2015
Allemandu, Seglolene, 'Crisis in Madagascar as Price of Vanilla
    Nears That of Gold', www.france24.com, 20 April 2018
Attokaran, Mathew, *Natural Food Flavors and Colorants*, 2nd edn
    (Chicago, IL, and Chichester, 2017)
Ayto, John, ed., *An A–Z of Food and Drink* (Oxford, 2002)
Baker, Aryn, 'Vanilla Is Nearly as Expensive as Silver: That Spells
    Trouble for Madagascar', http://time.com, 13 June 2018
Barrera, Laura Caso, and Mario Aliphat Fernández, 'Cacao,
    Vanilla, Annatto: Three Production and Exchange Systems
    in Southern Maya Lowlands, XVI–XVII Centuries', *Journal
    of Latin American Geography*, V/2 (2006), pp. 29–52
Barrett, Spencer C. H., 'The Evolution of Plant Sexual
    Diversity', www.nature.com, 2 April 2002
Bellis, Mary, 'The History of the Soda Fountain',
    www.thoughtco.com, 12 February 2019
Bomgardner, Melody M., 'The Problem with Vanilla',
    www.scientificamerican.com, 14 September 2016
Bory, Séverine et al., 'Biodiversity and Preservation of Vanilla:
    Present State of Knowledge', *Genetic Resources and Crop
    Evolution*, LV/4 (June 2008), pp. 551–71
Brillat-Savarin, Jean Anthelme, *Physiologie du Goût: Méditations
    de Gastronomie Transcendante* (Paris, 1841)
Brennan, Georgeanne, *Williams-Sonoma Salad of the Day: 365
    Recipes for Everyday of the Year* (San Francisco, CA, 2012)

Briscione, James, and Brooke Parkhurst, *The Flavor Matrix: The Art and Science of Pairing Common Ingredients to Create Extraordinary Dishes* (New York, 2018)

Bruman, Henry, 'The Cultural History of Vanilla', *Hispanic Historical Review*, XXVIII/3 (1948), pp. 360–76

Buccellato, F., 'Vanilla in Perfumery and Beverages', in *Handbook of Vanilla Science and Technology*, 2nd edn, ed. Daphna Havkin-Frenkel and Faith C. Belanger (Hoboken, NJ, and Chichester, 2011), pp. 37–8

Burton, James, 'The Leading Countries in Vanilla Production in the World', www.worldatlas.com, 1 February 2019

Cameron, Ken, *Vanilla Orchids: Natural History and Cultivation* (Portland, OR, and London, 2011)

Chambers, Alan, 'Potential for Commercial Vanilla Production in Southern Florida', https://crec.ifas.ufl.edu, 7 June 2018

Chin, Mei, 'Casanova: A Man's Healthy Appetite with All Life's Pleasures', www.irishtimes.com, 13 February 2018

Chow, Kat, 'When Vanilla Was Brown And How We Came to See it as White', www.npr.org, 23 March 2014

Collins, Maurice, *Cortés and Montezuma* (London, 1954)

Crosby Jr., Alfred, *The Columbian Exchange* (Westport, CT, 1992)

Curti-Diaz, Erasmo, *Cultivo y beneficiado de la vainilla en Mexico. Folleto technico para productores* (Papantla, Veracruz, 1995)

C. D., 'Why There Is a Worldwide Shortage of Vanilla', www.economist.com, 28 March 2019

Denn, Rebekah, 'Vanilla Extract Costs What? A Worldwide Shortage Means It's Time to Find Other Options', www.seattletimes.com, 4 September 2018

Ecott, Tim, *Vanilla: Travels in Search of the Ice Cream Orchid* (New York, 2004)

Endersby, Jim, *Orchid: A Cultural History* (Chicago, IL, and London, 2016)

Eurovanille, www.eurovanille.com/en

Evans, Meryle, 'The Vanilla Odyssey', *Gastronomica: The Journal of Critical Food Studies*, VI/2 (2006), pp. 91–3

'Extracts', www.mccormick.com, 8 March 2019

Feydeau, Elizabeth de, *Jean-Louis Fargeon, Parfumeur de Marie-Antoinette* (Versailles, 2005)

Food Non-Fiction, '#52 The Price of Vanilla', www.foodnonfiction.com, 19 May 2016

Fortini, Amanda, 'The White Stuff: How Vanilla Became Shorthand for Bland', https://slate.com, 10 August 2005

Foster, Lynn V., *Handbook to Life in the Ancient Maya World* (New York, 2002)

Funderburg, Ann Cooper, *Chocolate, Strawberry, and Vanilla: A History of American Ice Cream* (Bowling Green, OH, 1995)

Glasse, Hannah, *The Art of Cookery* [1747], www.archive.org, 11 July 2019

Havkin-Frenkel, Daphna and Faith C. Belanger, eds, *Handbook of Vanilla Science and Technology*, 2nd edn (New Brunswick, NJ, 2011)

Hernández-Hernández, J., 'Mexican Vanilla Production', in *Handbook of Vanilla Science and Technology,* 2nd edn, ed. D. Havkin-Frenkel and F. C. Belanger (Hoboken, NJ, 2011), p. 6

Hess, Mickey, 'Hip-Hop Realness and the White Performer', *Critical Studies in Media Communication*, XXII/5 (December 2005), pp. 372–89

Hoffman, Patrick G., and Charles M. Zapf, 'Flavor, Quality, and Authentication', in *Handbook of Vanilla Science and Technology*, 2nd edn, ed. D. Havkin-Frenkel and F. C. Belanger (Hoboken, NJ, 2011)

Innes, Hammond, *The Conquistadores* (London, 1969)

Jiménez, Álvaro Flores et al., 'Diversidad de Vainilla ssp. (Orchidaceae) y sus perfiles bioclimaticos en Mexico', *Revista de Biologia Tropical*, LXV/3 (September 2017), pp. 975–87

Kennedy, C. Rose, and Kaitlyn Choi, 'The Flavor Rundown: Natural vs Artificial Flavors', http://sitn.hms.harvard.edu, 21 September 2015

Kouri, Emilio, *A Pueblo Divided: Property and Community in Papantla, Mexico* (Stanford, CA, 2004)

Lanza, Joseph, *Vanilla Pop: Sweet Sounds from Frankie Avalon to ABBA* (Chicago, IL, 2005)

Laumer, John, 'Plain Vanilla Fail: A Matter of Climate
    Change, Population Growth, and Clear-cutting?',
    www.treehugger.com, 15 April 2012
Lohman, Sarah, 'The Marriage of Vanilla',
    www.laphamsquarterly.org, 4 January 2017
López de Gómara, Francisco, *Historia general de las Indias
    y Vida de Hernán Cortés* (Caracas, 1979)
Lubinsky, Pesach, Matthew Van Dam and Alex van Dam,
    'Pollination of Vanilla and Evolution in the Orchidaceae',
    Orchids, LXXV/12 (2006), pp. 926–9
—, et al., 'Origins and Dispersal of
    Cultivated Vanilla (Vanilla planifolia Jacks. Orchidaceae)',
    Economic Botany, LXII/2 (2008), pp. 127–38
McElveen, Ashbell, 'James Hemings, a Slave and Chef for
    Thomas Jefferson', www.nytimes.com, 4 February 2016
Medina, Javier De La Cruz, Guadalupe C. Rodriguez
    Jiménez and Hugo S. Garcia, 'Vanilla: Post-harvest
    Operations', www.fao.org, 16 June 2009
Odoux, Eric, and Michael Grisoni, eds, *Vanilla, Medicinal
    and Aromatic Plants – Industrial Profiles* (Boca Raton, FL,
    London and New York, 2010)
OEC World, https://oec.world/en/profile/hs92/0905,
    2 June 2019
Otterson, Joe, 'Vanilla Ice Laments Modern Music: "They
    Call This the Lost Generation"', www.thewrap.com,
    15 April 2016
Peck, Douglas T., 'The Geographical Origin and Acculturation
    of Maya Advanced Civilization in Mesoamerica', *Revista de
    Historia de America*, CXXX (2002)
Pilling, David, 'The Real Price of Madagascar's Vanilla Boom',
    www.ft.com, 4 June 2018
Powers, Karen, *Women in the Crucible of Conquest: The Gendered
    Genesis of Spanish American Society, 1500–1600* (Albuquerque,
    NM, 2005)
Rain, Patricia, *Vanilla Cookbook* (Berkeley, CA, 1986)
—, *Vanilla: The Cultural History of the World's Most Popular
    Flavor and Fragrance* (New York, 2004)

Ramirez, Santiago R. et al., 'Dating the Origin of the
    Orchidaceae from a Fossil Orchid with Its Pollinator',
    Nature, CDXL/7157 (30 August 2017)
Ranadive, A. S., 'Quality Control of Vanilla Beans and
    Extracts', in *Handbook of Vanilla Science and Technology*,
    2nd edn, ed. D. Havkin-Frenkel and F. C. Belanger
    (Hoboken, NJ, 2011), p. 145
Randolph, Mary, *The Virginian Housewife* (Baltimore, MD, 1824)
Reinikka, Merle A., *A History of the Orchid* (Portland, OR, 1995)
Risch, Sara J., and Chi-Tang Ho, eds, *Spices: Flavor Chemistry
    and Antioxidant Properties*, ACS *Symposium Series* 660
    (Oxford, 1997)
Rouhi, A. Maureen, 'Fine Chemical Firms Enable Flavor and
    Fragrance Industry', *Chemical Engineer News*, 14 July 2003,
    p. 54
Sawyer, Janet, *Vanilla: Cooking with One of the World's Finest
    Ingredients: Cooking with the King of Spices* (London, 2014)
Schwartz, Stuart B., *Victors and Vanquished: Spanish and Nahua
    Views of the Conquest of Mexico* (New York, 2000)
Sever, Shauna, *Pure Vanilla: Irresistible Recipes and Essential
    Techniques* (Philadelphia, PA, 2012)
Siegel, Matt, 'How Ice Cream Helped America at War',
    www.theatlantic.com, 6 August 2017
Smith, Andrew, ed., *The Oxford Encyclopedia of Food and Drink in
    America*, 2nd edn (Oxford, 2013)
Spector, Dina, 'The Twinkie Changed for Good Thanks to World
    War II', www.businessinsider.com, 17 November 2012
Spiegel, Alison, 'It's about Time You Knew Exactly Where
    Vanilla Comes From', www.huffpost.com, 6 November 2014
Stuckey, Maggie, *The Complete Spice Book* (New York, 1999)
Toledo, Victor M., et al., 'The Multiple Use of Tropical Forest
    by Indigenous Peoples in Mexico: A Case of Adaptive
    Management', *Conservation Ecology*, VII/3 (December 2003),
    pp. 1–17
Townsend, Camilla, 'Burying the White Gods: New Perspectives
    on the Conquest of Mexico', *American Historical Review*,
    CVIII/3 (June 2003), pp. 659–97

'Vanilla and Climate Change', www.vanille.com,
	17 February 2016
'Vanilla Extract', www.fda.gov, 2018
'Vanillas and Flavors', https://nielsenmassey.com, 2017
Young, James Harvey, 'Three Atlanta Pharmacists',
	Pharmacy in History, XXXI/1 (1989), pp. 16–17

Websites and Associations

Associations

American Orchid Society
www.aos.org

Kalapana Tropicals
www.kalapanatropicals.com

Laurence Hobbs Orchids
www.laurencehobbsorchids.co.uk

Odom's Orquids
www.odoms.com

The Orchid Society of Great Britain
www.osgb.org.uk

Royal Horticultural Society
www.rhs.org.uk

Société Française d'Orchidophilie
http://sfo-asso.fr

Western Kentucky Botanical Garden
www.wkbg.org

Information Source

u.s. Department of Agriculture
www.usda.gov

Purchasing Vanilla Beans, Extracts and Paste

Amazon
www.amazon.com

Elan Vanilla Company
www.elanvanilla.com/vanilla

Eurovanille
www.eurovanille.com/en/

Givaudan SA International Flavors & Fragrances
www.givaudan.com/flavours/world-flavours/vanilla

McCormick & Company
www.mccormick.com

Nielsen-Massey Vanillas, Inc.
https://nielsenmassey.com

Rodelle, Inc.
https://rodellekitchen.com/products/pure-vanilla-extract

Vanilla Pura
www.vanillapura.com

The Vanilla Queen
https://vanillaqueen.com/

The Watkins Company
www.watkins1868.com

Whole Foods Market
www.wholefoods.com

Williams-Sonoma
www.williams-sonoma.com/customer-service/
international-orders.html

Acknowledgements

I would like to thank the following individuals for their assistance while researching *Vanilla: A Global History*: Raul Garcia, Emma Singer, Nelson Santana and John Trigonis. Susan Lifrieri-Lowry, Thalia Pericles and Jean Claude for their delicious recipes. Anthony Smith, Tracy Zimmerman, Luz Espaillat-Dortrait, Lynette Dortrait, Luis Gallo and Leiry Gonzalez for proofreading. Philip Zeng for the graphics and Devir Shriky who formatted my pictures. Anne Martinez for testing my recipes. Julia Jordan, Elizabeth Schiable and Lynda Dias for their mentoring. Claire Stewart and Soley Velasquez Florez for supporting me throughout this process and to the faculty of New York City College of Technology, Hospitality Management Department.

I would also like to thank the New York Public Library, Ursula C. Schwerin Library and the CUNY Libraries for allowing me access to their databases and e-books.

Thank you to all who gave me confidence and moral support through this process.

Photo Acknowledgements

The author and publishers wish to express their thanks to the below sources of illustrative material and/or permission to reproduce it. Some locations are also given in the captions for the sake of brevity.

Photos aabbbccc/Shutterstock.com: pp. 27, 80; Ori Artiste/ Shutterstock.com: p. 16; photo Pierre-Yves Babelon/Shutterstock. com: p. 23; Biblioteca Nazionale Centrale, Florence: p. 44; photos Bouba: pp. 25, 58, 124; Casvero: p. 59; Château de Versailles: p. 50; from Norman Franklin Childers, *Vanilla Culture in Puerto Rico* (Washington, DC, 1948): p. 24; photo Clever Cupcakes: p. 70; from Betty Crocker, *Betty Crocker's Cook Book for Boys and Girls* (New York, 1957): p. 71; from *Curtis's Botanical Magazine*: pp. 12 (vol. CXXXI [4th Series, no. 1], 1905), 33 (vol. CVII [3rd Series, no. 47], 1891); from *Deutsche botanische Monatsschrift*, XXIII/12 (October, 1912): p. 45; photo Everett Collection/Shutterstock.com: p. 63; photo Everett Historical/ Shutterstock.com: p. 67; photo Everglades National Park (U.S. National Park Service): p. 17; photo FAMSI (Foundation for the Advancement of Mesoamerican Studies, Inc.): p. 44; photo Hitdelight/Shutterstock.com: p. 78; photo Brent Hofacker/Shutterstock.com: p. 34; from Franz Eugen Köhler, *Köhler's Medizinal-Pflanzen*, vol. II (Gera-Untermhaus, 1888–90): p. 15; photo Jay Lee/ Shutterstock.com: p. 22 (foot); photo Beirne Lowry: p. 74; from McCormick & Co., *Spices, their Nature and Growth; the Vanilla Bean; a Talk on Tea* (Baltimore, MD, 1915): p. 90; Metropolitan Museum of Art (Open Access): p. 35; National Portrait Gallery, London: p. 49;

Index